Mending the World
Spiritual Hope for Ourselves and Our Planet

Rev. Bruce G. Epperly
Rabbi Lewis D. Solomon

Innisfree
Press, Inc.
A call to the
deep heart's core

Published by Innisfree Press, Inc.
136 Roumfort Road
Philadelphia, PA 19119-1632
Visit our website at www.InnisfreePress.com.

Cover image "Gaia" © 2001 by Alice Kelley.
All Rights Reserved. www.alicekelley.com
Cover design by Hugh Duffy, PhD Design, Carneys Point, NJ.
www.phddesign.com

Library of Congress Cataloging-in-Publication Data
Epperly, Bruce Gordon.
Mending the world : spiritual hope for ourselves and our planet /
Bruce G. Epperly, Lewis D. Solomon.
p. cm.
Includes bibliographical references.
ISBN 1-880913-60-7
1. Spirituality. 2. Christianity and other religions—Judaism.
3. Judaism—Relations—Christianity. I. Solomon, Lewis D. II. Title.
BV4501.3.E67 2002
248—dc21
2002032893

Mending the World

We dedicate this book to our wives and spiritual partners,
Katherine Gould Epperly and Janet Stern Solomon.

A Word of Thanks

At the heart of the challenge to be God's partners in mending the world is the spirit of Shalom. The Hebraic word *Shalom* reminds us that we live in an intricate web of relationships, and that our well-being and creativity depend on the support and efforts of others. Accordingly, one of the greatest spiritual virtues is gratitude.

We would like to thank Rabbi Harold White for his pioneering work in interfaith spirituality and relationships. While others talk about interfaith dialogue, Rabbi White embodies this dialogue on a daily basis through his teaching, ministry, and innovative work in bringing persons of all faiths together in prayer and worship. We are grateful to our editor and publisher Marcia Broucek for her creative support and skillful editing. Sam Horn provided important guidance in style and communication during the early stages of this book.

I, Bruce, am grateful beyond words to Kate Epperly for her spiritual, professional, and personal partnership for the past twenty-five years. Her presence is found on every page. Matt Epperly provided challenge, love, and logistical support throughout the process of writing this book. From the very beginning, Patricia Farmer and Anna Rollins provided a wealth of encouragement, advice, and inspiration through their belief in this project and suggestions for the text. During the course of the writing, my father, Everett Epperly, died at age 91. Although he only vaguely knew about the project, his parenting was the foundation of my own spiritual journey and love of words. I am grateful for the impact of this gentle man of faith.

In addition to our gratitude to our wives and families, Lew and I would also like to thank the members of the Palisades Community Church in Washington, D.C., who generously invited us to share our ideas in an interfaith setting. Their ecumenical spirit embraces the insights of Jesus of Nazareth and the Jewish tradition from which he came.

—*Rosh Hashanah 2002 c.e./5763*

CONTENTS

CHAPTER ONE

Can These Dry Bones Live?

DO you know the tale of the lion cub that loses his mother and comes to live among goats? Years go by and the lion cub embraces the culture of the goat herd. Though majestic in appearance and stature, he eats grass, bleats like a goat, and runs in panic at the sound of the first threatening noise. He is secure only in the cramped universe of the goat herd. One day, however, the young lion's universe is turned upside down. As he meekly nibbles grass in the meadow, he is terrified by an unexpected sight. He bleats in fear and cowers trembling as the shadow of the great king of the forest falls upon him. He assumes that he will be dinner for the great lion king! To his amazement, the lion king ignores his cries, picks him up by his mane, and carries him to a nearby pond. As the great beast suspends the quivering young cub above the still waters, the king roars this challenge: "Look at your reflection. You are not a goat, you are a lion. Roar!"

This is our story—and the story of our faith traditions as well. Many of us have forgotten who we are. We settle for mediocrity when the universe needs artists, warriors, heroes, and heroines. Many of us forget that we are created in God's image and that the power of the universe is waiting to burst forth in our lives. We are spiritual lions who need a wake up call to discover who we are and claim the healing power that is our birthright and destiny. As God shows us the mirror of our lives, we see the reflection of a lion—a larger, more spiritual humanity within us. We catch a glimpse of wholeness and adventure within the harried and restless lives we often lead. The Eternal challenges us to claim our true reflection: "See yourself for what you are: a child of God with infinite potential." As God's beloved sons and daughters, we are meant for joy, abundance, and love. Even in difficult times, we can "roar," we can celebrate the wonder of our lives and the creative partnership to which God calls us.

This book is a testimony to this creative partnership. The authors of this book, a rabbi and a minister, met for the first time, when they were called upon to perform an interfaith wedding at the beautiful Dumbarton Oaks in Washington, D.C. As we enjoyed drinks and refreshments during the wedding reception, we discovered an amazing synchronicity in terms of our philosophy of life and spiritual journeys that became even more obvious in the writing of this book.

We share a passion for weaving together spirituality and healing in the face of personal and communal tragedy. We lament the tragic history of Jewish-Christian relations and ponder the possibility of an alternative future for these two great religious traditions. We hope to inspire a commitment to spiritual transformation among persons in churches and synagogues, as well as the millions of restless spiritual seekers of our time. To us, spirituality is dynamic, forward-looking, and open-ended. Faithfulness to God involves openness to the wisdom of other religions as well as the treasures of our own faiths. Like the prophets of the Hebrew tradition and the first Christian teachers, we imagine a spiritual reformation of Judaism and Christianity—a reformation in which these two religions become creative and supportive partners in addressing the personal and planetary spiritual needs of our times.

We realize that this creative partnership requires letting go of the painful personal and communal burdens of the past even as we envisage a transformed and transforming future for Judaism and Christianity. We cannot forget the horrors of history, but we also must look toward a future of mutual transformation and creative reconciliation between our faiths. That day in Dumbarton Oaks, we took the first steps in exploring a spiritual frontier to bring healing to both Christianity and Judaism, and wholeness to persons in search for something more than lifeless doctrines or empty consumerism. To the external observer, our meeting was purely accidental, but we continue to experience an amazing grace and surprising invitation from a Spiritual Presence beyond our conscious expectations. We believe that God is our guide and partner in this journey toward wholeness and reformation. We also believe that the spiritual practices that enable us to respond creatively to the challenges and tragedies of life can bring wholeness to our everyday lives and to the planet.

One of America's most famous short stories portrays the unintended adventure of a lazy Dutch farmer, Rip Van Winkle. One afternoon, as he meanders through the woods along the Hudson River hoping to avoid his daily chores, Rip encounters a group of strange men bowling amid the trees. He sits and drinks with them, and then falls into a deep slumber. When he finally awakens from his sleep, he discovers twenty years have passed. The British colonies have become the United States of America, George Washington has replaced King George as the national icon, and Rip's hard-working wife has died. Not to be daunted by twenty years of lost time, Rip moves in with his daughter and spends his remaining days as he had spent the first half of his life, gossiping and drinking on the porch of the local tavern. In twenty years, everything had changed except Rip Van Winkle's way of thinking. He had slept through a revolution. Sad to say, he continued to sleep through the revolutionary opportunities that were emerging with the formation of the new republic.

The dynamic and progressive spirit of Judaism and Christianity challenges us to wake up to our fullest potential. Yet, like Rip Van Winkle, many of us are sleeping through the revolutionary challenges going on within and around us.

Just think of the bold affirmations that are central to Judaism and Christianity:

- *"You are created in God's image."*
- *"You are the light of the world."*
- *"Your life is imprinted on the palm of God's hand."*
- *"God wants you to have abundant life."*
- *"God has a dream for your life."*

We are created for wholeness and abundance, and yet we live by scarcity and fear. We have forgotten that, just beneath the surface, our lives are a treasure trove of possibility, creativity, and growth. As the first century Jewish-Christian teacher Paul proclaimed, "Do not be conformed to this world, but be transformed by the renewing of your minds" (Romans 12:2).

A Chinese blessing/curse says, "May you live in interesting times." As we look at the spiritual landscape of our times, it is clear that these times are "interesting" for millions of seekers as well as for members of traditional religious faiths. Millions of people have committed themselves to a journey toward a wholeness of mind, body, and spirit that is global in scope. Within and beyond the church and synagogue, persons weave the traditional rituals and doctrines of their faiths into a tapestry that includes healing and spiritual practices such as T'ai Chi, ayurvedic medicine, acupuncture, Buddhist meditation, Gregorian chants, Jewish mysticism, Christian centering prayer, Zen meditation, Reiki touch healing, Native American sweat lodges, and herbal smudging. Many people fashion their own designer religions whose dimensions are cosmic rather than parochial in nature. Exploration and experience, rather than doctrine and ritual, characterize our personal spiritualities today.

Everywhere we turn, the image of reality in terms of isolated atoms and mind-body dualism is giving way to the holistic visions of the new physics and the new spiritual movements within and beyond traditional Judaism and Christianity. The current images of non-local causation, holograms, and ecological relatedness illumine the interdependence of body, mind, and spirit that transcends religious and ethnic boundaries. This emerging holism transforms our images of medicine and healing and revolutionizes the way we look at religion. It challenges us to explore innovative images of God and ourselves.

Today, ordinary persons are discovering extraordinary healing and wholeness. Confronted by life and death challenges of body, mind, and spirit, they are choosing life and discovering new and creative ways of living. Their journey may begin in a doctor's office with the news of a life-threatening illness, a memo announcing that a supposedly secure job has been eliminated as the result of a corporate merger or downsizing, a tragic accident, or an act of terrorism. But the path to healing may well lead them through prayer and meditation, Chinese medicine, healing touch, yoga, support groups, psychotherapy, therapeutic dance, dream work, and guided imaging. In partnership with other adventurers, more and more people are becoming the midwives and mapmakers of a whole new world of personal transformation. In the process, they are discovering spiritual hope for themselves and the planet.

Californians routinely grow up feeling earthquakes and their aftershocks and seeing houses sliding down mountainsides following heavy rainstorms. In the spirit of California's inherently unstable terrain, one bumper sticker proclaims, "Shift happens." That's the nature of reality. Life is constantly changing; the ground beneath our feet is continually shifting. Heraclitus, one of the earliest Greek philosophers, noted that "you can't step in the same waters twice." An upstart student corrected his master with the words "you can't even step in the same river once." Shift happens! Trying to hold on to what must eventually perish fills us with anxiety and sorrow. The apparent stability of life masks the deeper process of creation and destruction that characterizes our very existence. For many of us, twenty-first century life is like rafting in perpetual white water—personally, collectively as a nation, and globally. When the ground shifts beneath our feet, we can either run for cover and cling to old certainties, or let the shifts inspire us to new adventures of growth and creativity.

At forty-five, Susan's life had reached a spiritual and emotional standstill. Though she was a successful corporate attorney, her life was encompassed entirely by her career. Divorced and living by herself, Susan had few friends and barely saw her parents. Her sixty-hour work week left her little time to read, travel, play, or make new friends. Looking back, Susan recalls that though she was financially secure, her affluence could not take the place of a leisurely weekend hike along the Potomac River or a luncheon with a friend near her Washington, D.C. home. She felt empty and alone whenever she left the narrow technocratic confines of her legal profession. In her own mind, she had no identity apart from her career.

Without warning, one afternoon Susan began to experience chest pains and shortness of breath. "This can't be happening to me. I can't be having a heart attack," she remembers saying to herself. Always independent, Susan drove herself to the emergency room without bothering to consult her physician. On the way to the hospital, she asked herself whom she might call if she really *did* have a heart attack. Her ruminations shocked her. "Who would visit me? Who cares enough to help me in a time of need?" But, more troubling, she asked herself, "Who have *I* really befriended? Who have *I* supported in crisis?" The answers chilled her to the bone. Apart from her aging parents and her sister three thousand miles away, there was no one she could really turn to in a time of crisis.

The physicians confirmed that Susan, indeed, had experienced a heart attack. Though it was mild and did not leave any long-term damage, it was a spiritual and emotional wake-up call. Looking back at that time, Susan recalls saying to herself, "Something is truly wrong with my heart, and it involves more than physical vital signs. It involves a lack of friendship, love, and spirituality. Maybe I really do need a *heart* transplant. Maybe I need to start all over again. But, after all these years, how do I make a new start?"

As she thumbed through the Bible a friend had brought to the hospital, Susan came upon one of the Psalms. Something happened deep within her spirit as she read the words of Psalm 51:10: "Create in me a clean heart, O God, and put a new and right spirit within me."

Susan literally took those words to heart. She began to look at her life and examine her priorities. She knew she needed to exercise and watch her diet. But she needed something more than a technological fix or behavioral change. She needed a new heart and a new spirit. At forty-five, she embarked on a spiritual and relational training and exercise program. On the spur of the moment, she called an undergraduate professor who had impressed her with his free spirit and concern for his students. To her great joy, he remembered her and asked her to join him for coffee at the Student Union. Over the next several weeks, they met to talk about philosophy, study meditation, and examine what she needed to do to maintain her spiritual, emotional, and physical well-being. Inspired by their conversations, Susan began to meditate and pray regularly. After work, she chose to immerse herself in spiritual literature and the classics she had always meant to read, rather than the latest judicial decisions. Susan even began to take Saturdays off.

It was difficult at first, but Susan finally admitted to herself, "I work hard and aim at excellence, but I don't need to prove myself anymore. I can be a good attorney and still be a healthy and happy person." Slowly, she began to widen her circle of friends. She went on a number of Smithsonian tours and joined a book group sponsored by a local bookstore. She made herself available at no cost to elders in need of legal counsel and representation. She began to take time to get to know her parents and sister as friends, not just distant family members.

In response to a health crisis, Susan chose to embrace a new direction and learn new behaviors. She chose to awaken to her spirit. In mending her own heart, Susan chose to become one of God's partners in mending the world.

Susan is a pioneer of the spirit. But she is not alone in her journey. Countless adventurers of the spirit join East and West, mysticism and rationality, body and mind, and Judaism and Christianity in their quest for wholeness.

Nearly every day as we counsel interfaith couples or spiritual seekers, we hear the following confession: "I'm spiritual, but I'm not religious. I want to belong to a religious community for myself and my children, but I need a community that will teach me to pray, meditate, and deal with the stresses of life." In the minds of many seekers, religion and spirituality are simply incompatible with each other. To these seekers, religion is a set of confining and lifeless rules, irrelevant doctrines, and outmoded images of God and humankind. When they think of religion, they recall childhood feelings of guilt and shame, inspired by an image of a God who is out to punish the least infraction with hell-fire and brimstone. Spirituality, on the other hand, brings forth images of hope and transformation—freedom, creativity, growth, adventure, and the exploration of profound personal questions. Yet in a world of countless spiritual options, many seekers recognize that they do not have the resources for a solitary pilgrimage. They realize they need the support and insights of lively and inclusive spiritual communities in order to relate their individual spiritual insights to the challenges of everyday life and to foster a creative environment for their children. They yearn for a spiritual foundation that will enable them to face the storms of their personal lives.

Over twenty-five hundred years ago, the Hebraic prophet Ezekiel had a mystical vision of a valley of dry bones (Ezekiel 37:1-14). As Ezekiel saw he vast expanse of lifeless skeletons, God confronted him with the question, "Can these dry bones live?" Today, people within and outside traditional religious institutions ask the same question. We know the feelings of suffocation that dogmatic rules and confining fundamentalisms bring. But we live with the hope that new life can be breathed into old institutions and into the dryness of our own lives. We seek a path through the valley of dry bones that leads to vitality, adventure, and new creation, even for historic faiths such as Judaism and Christianity.

The path is a challenging one. Even as we dream of a lively partnership of progressive and inclusive Christians and Jews, we must confess the tragedies of the past. Without confession, we can never truly claim the surprising gifts of the present moment. While certain Jewish leaders may have persecuted the first Christians, certain Christians have for centuries sown the seeds of anti-Semitism that germinated into the fires of the Holocaust. Further, we mourn the religious persecution of scientific adventurers and spiritual innovators from the time of Jesus to our own day.

We believe that healing arises from the interplay of grief, confession, forgiveness, and hope, and that spiritual health arises from embracing our entire past, even that which was negative and life-destroying. Only after we have claimed the past in its fullness, can we forgive one another and embark on a journey of spiritual partnership. This inter-play of forgiveness and transformation applies to religious traditions as well as people.

Beyond forgiveness, we can experience the vitality that inspires a new vision of faith, spirituality, and partner-ship among Jews and Christians. This vitality emerges from affirming our common commitment to a dynamic, global spirituality as well as the unique gifts of each tradition. Yes, there is life in these dry bones! Christians and Jews to-gether, in true partnership, can reclaim the creative power of Shalom, God's wholeness of mind, body, and spirit. As we reclaim God's vision of Shalom, we bridge the chasm that lies between spirituality and religion, personal growth and social responsibility. Our faith will be intimate as well as planetary in nature. The spiritual imagination of the He-brew prophets and the compassion of Jesus will unite to bring healing to us as individuals, society, and the whole earth. These dry bones will rise as we commit ourselves to God's dream of mending the world.

Today, the concept of Shalom, which is the heart of Judaism and Christianity, is as vital and life-transforming as it was in the time of Hebraic prophets. The spirit of Shalom, by which Jesus and the Hebrew prophets lived and died, is multi-faceted and polyvalent in nature. It brings wholeness to every dimension of life. It creates community even as it inspires individual spiritual growth. It brings justice to the nation and the world, as well as health to the person. In a time in which challenge and change characterize our lives, awakening to the dynamic spirit of Shalom means that we embrace wholeness in every dimension:

Seven Gifts of Shalom

1. The healing of the whole person—mind, body, spirit, and relationships—through personal spiritual practices and communal rituals.

2. The joining of the right brain and left brain in rational analysis and intuitive visioning for personal transformation. Persons of Shalom are rational mystics whose visions and intuitive insights are woven together with the concreteness of everyday experience.

3. The uniting of ancient and modern spiritual visions to illuminate our ordinary lives.

4. Bringing together spirituality and medicine in a way that promotes individual and global healing.

5. Transforming Judaism and Christianity in partnership with each other for the purpose of renewing the vitality of each tradition.

6. Weaving together personal, social, and planetary well-being in an interrelated ecology of healing.

7. Finding God in the challenges of everyday experience. God's dream of Shalom proclaims that all things reveal the Holy.

Through the eyes of Shalom, the world is a Holy Adventure in which every encounter reveals the Divine for those who have eyes to see. Every nook and cranny is filled with God's presence. God's voice is heard in suffering as well as joy. The heavens declare the glory of God, and Divine inspiration can be experienced in our confrontation with acts of terrorism or the realities of bereavement and chronic illness.

When we embrace the spirit of Shalom, we become God's partners in mending the world. Old wounds are healed and new possibilities burst forth. Even in challenging times, we experience the companionship of a living and loving God and a lively community of caring friends. Shalom brings forth the healer and hero within each one of us. Shalom calls upon diverse religious traditions to heal their wounds and enter into creative partnerships in order to creatively transform persons and the planet. While life is difficult, we can discover the spiritual virtues and practices that will enable us to face tragedy with grace, dignity, and courage. While we may never understand evil, God's presence in our quest for wholeness will enable us to withstand and challenge the evils of our time.

The vision of Shalom awakens Christianity and Judaism from their spiritual slumbers and activates the powerful spiritual energies of these two faiths in partnership with one another. As the wounds of history are healed and transformed, Christians and Jews have the opportunity to discover that, despite their differences, they are united by fundamental life-changing affirmations. The unique gifts of each tradition can enrich one another as we claim our place as partners in the quest for God. Christians will continue to affirm the centrality of Jesus as God's revelation of Divine love and creativity. Jews will continue to embrace the vision of the Messianic era when we will serve as partners with God in perfecting the world. But together, we will discover our wholeness as spiritual siblings whose task is to enlighten and heal humankind. In companionship with one another, we will discover the lively presence of God that gave birth to both faiths and inspires our openness to transformation in the twenty-first century.

At the heart of the spirit of Shalom is a shared vision

of reality, grounded in the following seven life-changing af-firmations. These affirmations reveal the lively spiritual partnership that unites Christianity and Judaism in an age of quantum physics and religious pluralism. These affirmations are as ancient as the Hebrew prophets and the teachings of Jesus, and as contemporary as the wisdom gained from medical studies on the positive health benefits of spiritual commitment and the insights of the new physics.

Seven Life-Changing Affirmations

1.   *Life is good and the world is beautiful.*

Created by the Holy One, all things reflect Divine creativity, intelligence, and love. While the world is not perfect, it is essentially and inherently good. Our bodies, minds, and relationships reflect Divine wholeness at every level. The Eternal One is right where we are, speaking to us through the voice of a spouse, friend, or child, and in the wind that caresses our cheek.

2.   *God's love and creativity is our deepest reality.*

God created humankind in the Divine image. As God's sons and daughters, we are of infinite and eternal value. Divine intelligence and beauty shine through our lives regardless of our current life situation. Divine possibility and adventure are our birthright and our future. We can experience God's companionship and guidance in every situation. Everywhere we look, we can see a child of God whose beauty penetrates even the most distressing disguise. Each of us is that child, and God has given us all we need to face life's challenges. We can roar in joyful creativity and self-affirmation.

3. *Love God in the world of the flesh.*

There is no need to escape the world of the flesh in order to find God. The planet is an icon of Divine love and creativity that calls us to the gentle care and nurture of all things. The body is beautiful and reflects God's eternal and ever-present beauty. Sexuality and parenting are sacred gifts to be enjoyed and nurtured. The non-human world is to be cherished as a companion in our earthly adventure. We love God by loving our neighbors and the stranger as well as the non-human world.

4. *Life is adventurous and surprising.*

The biblical stories center on personal and communal pilgrimages. As the children of Abraham and Sarah, the pilgrims of the Exodus and the adventurous Ruth and Naomi, and the disciples of Jesus who explored the Roman world, we are challenged to stretch our own spiritual frontiers. God constantly calls us to new horizons of the spirit and flesh. Faithfulness to the Holy One involves the transformation as well as affirmation of the past in light of the emerging and uncertain future. We can respond creatively to every life situation, even illness and death, no matter how tragic. Beyond every death is the promise of the immortal soul and new life.

5. *God is with us and within us inspiring and guiding us in every situation.*

God speaks to us in "sighs too deep for words" (Romans 8:26). The Holy Adventure wells up from within us, constantly presenting us with possibilities for growth and new life. While the Eternal One is not confined to our world, the Divine Center is active everywhere as the intimate wellspring of life and love. We are never alone. God is with us, sharing our joy and pain, and bringing beauty out of difficult situations. Divine inspiration is ours, if we have ears to hear and eyes to see.

6. *We can choose to become partners with God in creating a world of love and beauty.*

Like a good parent, God wants us to discover our unique gifts and possibilities. The Holy One delights in the creative use of freedom. The All-Loving God enjoys a good surprise and constantly pushes us beyond our comfort zones so we can embody God's own aim at beauty. We can become co-creators of a world of beauty, love, and justice. We are called to bring eternal wisdom to everyday life by becoming the creators, artists, and healers of ourselves in partnership with God and all creation.

7. *God is the source of novel possibilities that enable us to face evil, tragedy, illness, aging, and death with a vision of hope and wholeness.*

Nothing can separate us from God's love. Even in "the darkest valley" (Psalm 23:4) we can encounter the living God who shares our pain and rejoices in our growth. While we cannot always choose the circumstances of our lives, with God as our companion and friend, we can find wholeness in life. We can find meaning and beauty even in the most challenging situations.

❀

A television commercial invites viewers to taste a particular cereal again "for the first time." This is our invitation to you. Taste and see that there is something new and unexpected in the partnership of progressive and inclusive Christians and Jews. As artists of the spirit, we weave together a vision of life in all its abundance that embraces ancient wisdom and modern science, prayer and quiet meditation, human creativity and Divine possibility, personal growth and planetary well-being.

Just as our meeting and writing this book together is not accidental, your reading of it is not entirely a matter of chance. We are all part of an intricately connected spiritual adventure that calls us to look at ourselves, our spirituality, and the world in novel and unprecedented ways. We invite you to become participants in the creative transformation of society and the planet. Awaken to this new world of adventurous spirituality. Let the timeless, yet always novel, vision of Shalom be your guide into a world of adventure and wholeness.

Shalom!

CHAPTER TWO

God, Where Are You When I Need You?

SCOTT Peck begins his best-selling book, *The Road Less Traveled*, with the words "life is difficult." Indeed, in spite of the legendary Garden of Eden or the myths of a Golden Age, life has been challenging from the very beginning. Scientific research reveals that the experience of pain emerged with the dawn of humanity. Archeologists have discovered broken bones, malnutrition, and even tooth decay among the first humans. The biblical story of Adam and Eve reflects the experience of every human being: Sooner or later, we are driven out of the garden of innocence. Whether the cause is the evil acts of others, our own actions, the impact of parental choices, or economic factors, we are left, like the legendary first couple, to pick up the pieces. We must either move on with our lives or find ourselves crippled by our responsibility for the pain of the world and the burden of our own pain. Like the first humans, we must deal with the reality of sickness, death, and violence.

For many of Bruce's first-year students at Georgetown University, September 11, 2001, challenged their vision of themselves and the future. Blissfully innocent in the adventure of the first weeks of college life, the attacks on the Pentagon and the World Trade Center shattered their sense of trust and security and clouded their images of the future. As they viewed the smoke of the Pentagon just a few miles across the Potomac, they discovered the truth of Martin Luther's observation that "in the midst of life, we are surrounded by death." With the collapse of the World Trade Center, their naïve confidence in the future was broken. In the weeks that followed the attacks on America, many of them asked, "Where is God in this tragedy? Does God have a plan for our world and our own lives? Will God be with me when I face failure and tragedy?" Many were angry at a God who could allow such evils to occur. Others wondered, "In the face of all this death and destruction, do my small problems matter to God or the universe?"

Since September 11th, the words of Psalm 46:2-3, "the mountains shake in the heart of the sea" and "waters roar and foam," have become a reality for countless Americans. Despite the counsel of national leaders, life may never be "normal" again for this generation. Like those diagnosed with life-threatening cancer or abused by their spouse, normalcy is an illusion. Still, we ask ourselves and the universe, can we discover something constant and abiding when the foundations of our lives have been shaken? In the midst of death, can we experience the deeper forces of life that stand firm regardless of the pain or fear that threatens to overwhelm us? In such moments, many of us cry out, "God, where are you when I need you?"

We must each eventually face pain and suffering on our own. No one can live or die for us, nor can anyone fully banish the anguish that is the destiny of all mortals. Yet our encounter with pain and suffering can be the catalyst for personal destruction or for spiritual growth. We can discover life's meaning and God's companionship not by denying the suffering of the world and our pain, but by embracing our own despair with courage and hope.

"Why Me? Why NOT Me?"

Each of us confronts suffering differently. For Andrew, life was going well until he was diagnosed with an inoperable brain tumor. A successful executive, he felt invulnerable until that fateful day when the test results came back. No longer defined by his financial success, he was now just another vulnerable, frightened, and lonely patient, endlessly waiting for one procedure after another. While he had not attended temple since his bar mitzvah, the diagnosis immediately plunged Andrew into questions that he had previously ignored as far too abstract for a person of science and rationality to consider. As he pondered his future, his mind moved from questions of personal mortality to cosmic justice. In the wee hours of the morning when sleep eluded him, he asked himself over and over again, "What have I done to deserve this fate? Is God punishing me for some improper business dealing that I unknowingly committed? Is the cancer a result of my decision to turn my back on my faith?" But then he also asked, "Do I really deserve this pain and this premature death? Is this justice? Am I being condemned to disability and death just because I focused too much on financially supporting my family and spent too little time with them? I've been a good man, haven't I? This isn't right. I don't deserve this!"

This same experience of the mystery of pain and suffering was at work in Stephanie's attitude toward the series of incidents that prevented her from boarding a plane that eventually crashed, killing everyone on board. On the morning of the departure, Stephanie lost her car keys and couldn't find her spare key ring. Afraid she would miss her flight, she anxiously searched her home until she found the missing keys. When she tried to start her car, she found to her anger that her battery was dead. "This day started off bad, and it's only getting worse," she muttered to herself. "What will be next?" Luckily, she hailed a cab on the busy thoroughfare near her home. She was certain she could make her flight until the cab was caught in a traffic jam created by a car accident on the freeway. Angry and frustrated, Stephanie finally took a later flight. When she arrived at her destination, she was shocked to hear that the flight she had intended to take crashed due to an equipment failure. As she related the story to friends, some glibly responded, "It just wasn't your time." Others consoled her with the words, "It wasn't God's will for you to die" or "You must be on good terms with God." One even joked, "Remember what Billy Joel says, only the good die young." Still others saw her escape from death as God's challenge for her to change her life.

Although Stephanie appreciated all these gestures of support, she was troubled by their deeper meaning. "Does God really have a plan for my life? What about the others? Were their lives meaningless? Was my being late for the plane Divine providence, accident, or fate? Did God hide my keys and ruin my battery just to save my life? Didn't God care for the others enough to protect them? Why didn't God give them an opportunity to change their lives?" Though she was grateful for her survival, Stephanie had trouble thanking God for the near miss. She reflected, "I just can't forget the faces of the plane crash victims on television or their grieving relatives. It could have been me. My relatives could have been the ones mourning my death. I'm no better than they were. Why wasn't I on the plane?"

Although Stephanie still finds the apparent synchronicity that lead to missing the plane flight a mystery, she has changed her life. Today, she volunteers regularly in a home for battered women. She tells her friends and family how much she loves them and seizes each precious moment as an opportunity to share the joy of living. Although her near miss challenged her to commit herself to reaching out to others, Stephanie still feels uneasy with her survival, and she scorns the platitudes people recite to make sense of her narrow escape. She wonders about the person who may have gotten her seat on the flight or the passenger who might have sat next to her on that fateful day. She ponders whether there was some hidden Divine plan working beneath the inconveniences of that fateful day. As she reads about similar plane crashes or persons her age dying of cancer or heart disease, she sometimes asks herself, "Why not me? What saved me? What's so special about my life that I was set apart from the others?"

No doubt, many of the people who changed travel plans, left the office to go out for a walk, or decided to stay home from work on September 11th feel the same way. Intensely grateful for the gift of life, they wonder about the synchronous events and decisions that kept them away from the World Trade Center or the Pentagon that fateful morning.

The question of suffering is as old as the biblical story of Job. According to the rules of his faith community, Job had done everything right. He deserved success and a long, pain-free life. His faith identified success with holiness and good behavior. Conversely, failure and sickness were seen as the result of sin and disobedience. Pious and ethical to a fault, Job's life went along perfectly until the day a storm toppled his house, killing his children, the market collapsed, and his herds were destroyed. Worse still, he contracted a skin disease that made his life a living hell. Once, Job believed that pain and suffering always happened to other people, and that when tragedy came upon them, they deserved it. Now, Job was suffering the same indignities that he previously identified as Divine punishment for sin. Job's view of Divine justice and personal security were shattered. He cried out in anguish and confusion to the Eternal One, "What have I done wrong? Surely I have not been bad enough to lose everything—children, home, wealth, and health. I don't deserve this!" Thinking himself to be righteous, Job complained to God, "You've changed the rules of the game. Is there no justice in life? How can righteous suffer when the evil die happily in their sleep, rested and well-fed? It's just not fair."

In one interpretation of the Book of Job, Job's complaints were silenced when God showed him how insignificant his place was in the divinely created universe. God's care extends to the stars and the sea creatures, not just to individual human beings. Job had to see his life in the context of the cosmos as a whole and not just his own little corner of the universe. "Where were you when I laid the foundation of the earth?" asked God (Job 38:4). Even though sections of the universe may appear frayed, the whole tapestry of life is beautiful in God's eyes.

In his alternative interpretation of the story, Rabbi Harold Kushner suggests that there are simply certain events that God cannot prevent. Like ourselves, God must also contend with chaos, accident, and misused freedom. There is no linear one-to-one correspondence between morality and health. In a world of chance, pain and suffering cannot be avoided, but they can be redeemed through compassion toward our neighbors and partnership with God.

If we read Job's narrative carefully, we discover that Job's story is our own. As sages have long reminded us, pain and suffering is the lot of all who are born. Eventually each of us will bury our parents, face tragedy and serious illness, experience physical or mental disability, and contemplate our own immanent deaths—that is, if we live long enough! We may face loss of employment, divorce, alienation from a beloved child, or the death of a spouse. While some persons are overwhelmed with one death after another and the diagnosis of a serious illness all in a brief period of time, others manage to escape death and suffering until later in life or experience pain and bereavement spread out over a long time span. Still, eventually each one of us will struggle with our own pain and the suffering of those we love.

But the mystery of pain and suffering goes beyond our individual experience. As Americans, we wonder, "Where was God at Littleton or Oklahoma City or the World Trade Center?" But we are not alone in our anger and grief. Parents in Afghanistan, Israel, and Palestine ask the same question of the Eternal One following the explosion of a land mine, a suicide bombing, or a stray bullet from a soldier.

We recognize moral evil when we see it. But we still ask, "How can humans be so evil? Why can't God make us more loving?" We think of the massive political evils of the past two centuries. We have seen the legacy of slavery, as well as the genocide of Native Americans, and the tragic impact these social evils have left in inner-city ghettoes and rural reservations. Beyond our shores, in this most enlightened age, we have witnessed the Armenian genocide, African tribal warfare, purges in Russia and China, unending conflict between Jews and Palestinians, ethnic cleansing in the former Yugoslavia, and the Holocaust. Where was God when countless innocent persons died in places like Auschwitz, Buchenwald, Liberia, Jonestown, and the World Trade Center? Where is God in the cancer ward and the psychiatric unit? Why does a good and loving God allow so much pain and anguish? Does suffering have any value for ourselves or those we love?

Our naïve images of human spiritual evolution are shattered when we confront the diabolical actions of nations and individuals in our time. With Woody Allen, we wonder whether or not God is an "underachiever" in the creation and ongoing maintenance of the world. While the answers to these questions draw us toward the Great Mystery, we still seek solace and a vision of reality that will give us courage in life's most difficult moments.

As we ponder the relationship of God and suffering, it is important to distinguish between pain and suffering. Medically speaking, pain is a purely physical signal, telling us that something is wrong. Like the oil and temperature gauges on a car dashboard, the experience of pain is often a wake-up call to seek medical care or change our life. In that regard, pain may be a factor in maintaining our overall physical, emotional, and spiritual well-being. The pain of childbirth or running a marathon may be unpleasant at times, but we seldom see it in terms of suffering and evil. Something good will come of birth pangs, and muscle aches are a sign of our physical well-being. When we see our pain from a larger perspective, we recognize that certain pain is ironically "good for us."

Still, pain and suffering are so closely linked that we seldom distinguish one from the other. Chronic physical and emotional pain eventually leads to the experience of suffering and to the recognition that our personal wholeness is in jeopardy. Suffering often involves the experience of isolation, fear, anguish, and woundedness of body, mind, and spirit. We can never underestimate the power of pain to overwhelm us entirely, making our lives a living hell, even making suicide and euthanasia attractive methods of pain relief. Although we cannot escape suffering, still we seek a reason for our suffering and, more importantly, we seek a way to find meaning and spiritual growth in the inevitable suffering of life.

"Why Is There Suffering?"

The experience of pain and suffering makes theologians of all of us. Even if we have no formal theological education and scorn the ethereal abstractions of religious language, we still attempt to make sense of the world and the accidents that threaten our well-being. When we seek a reason for the suffering we experience, we typically look in three directions for an answer: the acts of God, the results of our own behaviors, and the impact of the many-faceted world within which we live. Here are some common, even popular, views that try to explain the suffering in our world:

1.   *"It's God's will."*

God is the first place we go in our quest to find meaning in, as well as deliverance from, suffering. Popular religion asserts that there must be a reason for everything. In our search for a reason, God seems the best candidate since the Eternal is the creator of all things. God sets up the rules and metes out the punishments, according to facile religious explanations.

The simplest explanation for suffering is the belief that everything that happens reflects God's will, that nothing exists without God's expressed permission or action. Not a leaf falls, plane crashes, or cancer cell proliferates apart from God's activity. Whatever happens—from AIDS to acts of terror—comes directly or indirectly from the hand of Almighty God. The Eternal One is the force that directly or indirectly motivates the diabolical actions of terrorists who hijack an airplane as well as the selfless compassion that inspires firefighters and police officers to risk their lives to save others. People with this view cite the Scripture, "I force light and create darkness. I make weal and create woe" (Isaiah 45:7).

In its most radical form, embodied by the John Calvin, this view holds that God predestines every event without exception. If we are saved, it's entirely God's doing. But if we are damned to an eternity of suffering, this is also God's doing. To those who challenge this view of God's unilateral power, the faithful respond that the Eternal is in sovereign control, and we are nothing. Apart from God's omnipotent will, we would not exist. God is the potter, we are the clay. Can the clay complain to the potter about the shape of the dish or bowl? If God decides to break the bowl with cancer, heart disease, a terrorist's bomb, financial ruin, or genocide, there is nothing we can really do or say about it. From this viewpoint, all we can do is submit to whatever the Eternal One wills without question. Questioning God's will is a sign of faithlessness that may lead to Divine punishment.

In the name of this omnipotent God, some have claimed justification of horrific crimes. Some have justified their cruelty by affirming that they are empowered instruments of Divine sovereignty sent to civilize the pagan, eliminate the Christ killer, bomb the abortion clinic, or destroy the infidel. These conquerors see themselves as the chosen vehicles for God's "manifest destiny" and "holy will."

2.   *"It's for your own good."*

Others try to rescue God's goodness by suggesting that the pain and suffering of this world is really "for your own good." According to this view, God is interested in developing persons of character, strength, and stature. They take the stance that a world without conflict or challenge would bring about weak and amoral creatures, that suffering and evil give us authentic opportunities to grow ethically and spiritually. They believe that God, like an athletic coach, sets obstacles in our way in order to promote human achievement. In light of September 11th, many people cite the rise in patriotism, unity, and compassion in America, as well as the growing partnership among nations committed to eliminating terrorism, as justifying God's permission of the terrorist acts. They believe that, from this evil, God is seeking a greater good that will far outweigh the death of a few thousand and the grief of their families.

Some see suffering as a lesson aimed at our spiritual growth. When three boys died in a car crash following a night of partying, for example, one pious observer was heard to say, "Their deaths are not in vain. This will teach other teens not to drink and drive." People who take this stance believe that tragedy may be needed to get the point across, that the sufferings inspire us to change our lives and prevent greater evils from occurring. From their viewpoint, the world is a better place and we are stronger persons because of the suffering we experience.

3.   *"That's the way it is. There's nothing I can do about it."*

For some, God is the Zeus-like, power-hungry wielder of thunderbolts. For others, God is simply absent from all human affairs. From this viewpoint, God is the metaphysical "first cause," the great watchmaker who gets things started and then disappears, letting history take its course with little or no interference. We're on our own in a universe that neither hears our prayers nor responds to our cries for help.

Probably the most popular Divine image combines the emotional distance of the absent parent with the ruthless power of the absolute monarch. Dwelling on high, immune to human suffering and pain, this God resembles the proverbial "Saturday's father." Unconcerned with the tasks of ordinary life, this God intervenes with mighty acts of healing and destruction in response to the right kind of prayers or the wrong kind of behavior. While some persons take comfort in a God who acts supernaturally from the outside, this disconcerting view holds that God is ultimately arbitrary and inconsistent, showing up, frankly, when not needed and absent when needed most. While dramatic interventions leave us breathless, most of the time we are left alone without guidance or support. This absent God has left us with a spiritual instruction book, but the one-dimensional pages of Scripture don't calm our fears or feed our dreams with the care that we need in a relationship with a constant, trustworthy, and loving companion. This God leaves the world of ordinary life—the everyday life of relationships, parenting, work, aging, and chronic illness—virtually godforsaken.

Absent, omnipotent, or arbitrary, these popular of God share one thing in common: They hold that God's relationship to the world is one-sided. God influences the world, but is never truly influenced by the world. God gives but never receives. God demands but never listens. The Eternal loves the chosen ones, but only on the Divine terms. Like the narcissistic parent, this kind of Divine love centers on its own desires and not the authentic needs of the child. We are neither valuable nor lovable in our unique selves, but are interesting to God only as we are extension of God's will for us. If we have freedom and creativity at all in relationship to the Eternal, it adds nothing to our Creator's joy or satisfaction. Instead, our scientific, medical, and intellectual creativity is a threat to this egocentric potentate who may unleash hell-fire and brimstone if we become too adventurous or too creative. This God demands obedience and submission, or else!

Tragically, some religious leaders have sacrificed the vision of God's love before this throne of arbitrary and unilateral power. They have assumed that ambiguous and arbitrary power is more intellectually satisfying than an ever-present love that may include failure and uncertainty for both ourselves and for God. To these traditionalists, Divine power must be either absolute or nonexistent. There is no middle ground. God must ultimately determine the totality of life or be ineffectual and absent from the affairs of the universe. But the God who is defined primarily in terms of power and might cannot help us in our misery, for our despair has come from that God's hand.

4.   *"It's all your fault."*

When they observed a man who had been blind from birth, Jesus' disciples asked him, "Who sinned, this man or his parents?" (John 9:2). They believed that there must be a reason for a lifetime of blindness, and the reason must be in the misdeeds of humans before their birth or the actions of their parents.

Historically, many people have substituted the omnipotent mind for the omnipotent God. New age spirituality states that we create our own realities. New age healers assert that we are responsible for everything that happens in our lives—our relationships, health, financial well-being, and life span. Success and failure are completely in our hands. Positive thinking and imaging eventually bring health, wealth, and happiness, while negativity inevitably leads to illness, poverty, and depression.

When Claire was diagnosed with multiple sclerosis, her new age spiritual guide asked, "What have you done to bring this illness upon yourself?" After Claire's use of affirmations and imagery did not bring a remission, this same spiritual guide challenged her, "Why are you holding on to this illness? What negative thoughts are dominating your mind?" Claire felt helpless and guilt-ridden, and her feelings of guilt contributed to further symptoms of multiple sclerosis. The omnipotent mind, whose power was meant to save her, only further imprisoned her in guilt and self-doubt. She felt she couldn't even share her concerns with her new age friends because she knew that they would judge her negative thinking and might even avoid her for fear that her negativity might impede their own spiritual progress. In their philosophy, if you are suffering, it must be your fault. You created the reality of pain and suffering, and only you can get yourself out of it.

Many new age thinkers unite the Eastern doctrine of karma with Western optimism. The doctrine of karma simply says you reap what you sow, that the universe within which we live reflects our state of mind and behaviors from life to life. From this perspective birth defects, child abuse,

AIDS, and impoverished childhoods are not accidental or random, but manifest the energy we take from life to life. Genius, wealth, and birth into a healthy family equally reflect the impact of our previous lifetimes. Our experience of pain and suffering of body, mind, and spirit reflects our need to learn spiritual lessons that we neglected in a previous lifetime. When we learn this particular lesson in our soul's curriculum, we can move on to the next stage in our spiritual evolution. In the soul's journey, the operation of personal and cosmic karma is purely neutral. The impersonal workings of inexorable cause and effect provide no love or support for persons in pain. Each must work out their own healing and salvation on their own. We must transform our minds by ourselves.[1]

Although evangelical Christians see the idea of karma as a heresy that centers on human activity rather than Divine grace and omnipotence, many evangelicals do affirm a linear cause-and-effect relationship between imperfection and suffering that closely resembles the karmic justice affirmed by Asian and new age thinkers. In the wake of September 11th, for example, some religious leaders have suggested that the terrorist actions reflected God's withdrawal of protection of America for its acceptance of homosexuality, paganism, and abortion. While often touted as orthodox in certain Christian circles, this doctrine implies that God is a judge out to get us and our children for the slightest infraction. This view connects missing church with a car accident. If we don't pray enough, we will suffer the consequences. God, this argument runs, bears grudges for

---

1   For a more detailed discussion of this position, see Bruce Epperly, *Crystal and Cross: Christians and the New Age in Creative Dialogue* (Mystic, CT: Twenty Third Publications, 1996).

the slightest sin that will eventually lead to disaster for our children and children's children.

Following a lecture, a middle-aged man approached Bruce with tears in his eyes. He told the story of the final painful weeks of his daughter's life. As his daughter lay dying of cancer, a pious Christian lady advised that if he and his wife only trusted God and prayed more diligently, she would recover. He felt both guilt and anger as he looked back on his daughter's final days. Could his prayers really have made a difference? Would she still be alive if he had trusted God more? In this belief system, the victim is responsible for her or his fate, or the well-being of her or his loved ones.

Grounding their theology in the biblical Book of Leviticus, people of the reward-punishment calculus persuasion assert that we deserve what we receive at the hands of a just God. They believe that the Eternal rewards the faithful, that the righteous will be blessed with wealth, power, and long life. In contrast, the evil doers will reap punishment for their misdeeds, and God will punish them from generation to generation. They take the words of the Book of Leviticus literally:

> If you follow my statutes and keep my commandments and observe them faithfully, I will give you your rains in their season, and the land shall yield its produce. . . . you shall eat your bread to the full, and live securely in your land. . . . I will look with favor upon you and make you fruitful . . . I will bring terror on you; consumption and fever that waste the eyes, and cause life to pine away. . . . I will set my face against you, and you shall be struck down by your enemies. (Leviticus 26: 3-4, 5, 9b, 14, 16-17)

These linear cause-and-effect, reward-punishment visions of suffering and success ultimately blame the victim and leave people with a religion ruled by guilt rather than love. A humorous example of this tendency occurred in an interchange between Bruce's wife, Kate, and one of her best friends, a "recovering" Roman Catholic. When she saw that her friend's sole had a hole in it, Kate innocently remarked, "Susie, there's something wrong with your sole." To which her friend replied, "Oh, no, not my soul! What have I done wrong now?"

5.   *"It's the Devil's fault."*

There are strands of both Judaism and Christianity that see suffering as the result of the eternal struggle between good and evil, often personified through images of the ongoing warfare between God and Satan. According to the mystical thinker Rabbi Isaac Luria, before God created the world, the Eternal One left a space for human creativity. The process of creation itself involved the clash of the polar powers of mercy and judgment. This primordial conflict left in its wake an evil residue, reflected in the dark shells covering what once were perfect vessels of Divine light. These shells mask the true reality of the soul as a spark of Divine light. God's initial withdrawal from the universe enables people to exercise free will in going from darkness to light and choosing to become partners with God in improving and completing the world. But God's withdrawal also makes suffering and evil possible for mortal beings. By implication, it also creates the context in which superhuman forces of evil might also emerge.

Orthodox Christianity often invokes the fallen angel, Satan, popularly called the Devil, as the ultimate ground of evil and suffering. Rather than aligning himself with God's benevolent plan for creation, Satan used his freedom to turn away from God. Satan chose the path of self-centered power rather than benevolent love. While God seeks abundant life for all things, Satan seeks to lure creation away from the wholeness that comes from authentic partnership with God and love for one's neighbor. Diabolical in nature, Satan is the ground of the division, war, alienation, and hatred we experience as individuals and as members of the human community.

Satan's interventions are seen as the source of the sin and alienation that eventually manifests itself in violence, disease, and death. Many consider Satan the force behind the Holocaust, the widespread practice of abortion, and even American foreign policy. Throughout the centuries and even today in certain conservative Christian circles, mental illness, cancer, car accidents, and assassinations are seen as evidence of Satan's diabolical presence in human life. Accordingly, the actions of the terrorists on September 11th have been labeled as Satanic by certain Christian fundamentalists. Ironically, the demonic has also been seen as the source of American imperialism by certain Muslim fundamentalists who believe the terrorists' actions were instruments of Divine justice. This world view asserts that, in the battle between God and Satan, we are helpless victims of powers beyond ourselves. With the comedian Flip Wilson, we protest our mistakes with the words, "The Devil made me do it."

6.   *"It's all their fault!"*

Many people see themselves as the victims of forces beyond their control that determine their lives. From this perspective, the universe is a dynamic web of relationships whose impact limits and shapes human experience and choices. Whether their lives are shaped by genetic inheritance and DNA, social and family conditioning, ethnicity, or gender, they feel themselves at the mercy of forces they did not create. Instead of invoking God, karma, or personal freedom as the source of suffering, they give up their power to the natural, environmental, and filial forces that give life and, for good or ill, continue to condition their lives.

From this viewpoint, illnesses such as spina bifida, cancer, or Lou Gehrig's disease are neither chosen at the soul level, nor are they dispensed by an arbitrary God, but they simply arise in the apparently accidental interplay of DNA, molecules, cells, and environmental influences. Ultimately, we are victims of malevolent natural forces beyond our control. The best we can do is simply to endure the pain until a pharmaceutical, therapeutic, or surgical remedy comes along.

A Transformative View of Suffering

Our experience challenges, yet embraces, certain aspects of these explanations of suffering: the actions of an omnipotent God; the choices of an all-determining mind; the forces of evil; and the passivity of an impotent self before its genetic or environmental heritage. From our perspective, God cannot be both all-powerful and all-loving, as these words are traditionally understood. While no words can fully describe the Eternal One, the deepest words of the biblical tradition point to a God whose power is embodied in love and companionship rather than coercion and emotional withdrawal. In the spirit of Shalom, we offer the following perspectives of a fully personal and intimate God:

1.   *God is a comforting, caring presence in our lives.*

The God we affirm is intensely personal and caring. We believe God has a tender care for all creatures, human and non-human. We are imprinted on God's hand. The Loving One has numbered the hairs of heads and breathes within each one of us. God rejoices in our joy and inspires our creativity. As Jesus of Nazareth proclaimed, the breadth of Divine love includes the lilies of the fields and the birds of the air as well as society's forgotten ones (Matthew 6:25-33; Matthew 25:31-40). Like a good parent, God enjoys surprise, freedom, and novelty. Our Promethean discoveries bring Divine affirmation rather than angry thunderbolts. The Holy One is not aloof but ever-present as our companion and guide. The God who mothers and fathers us all guides us moment by moment, luring us toward our fullest humanity through dreams, intuitions, synchronous encounters, gentle inclinations. When we are walking through the valley of the shadow of death, the Eternal One is our companion, comfort, and guide. Evil and suffering cannot destroy us because God is truly with us!

While images of Divine punishment and anger abound in the Bible, we see these as imperfect representations of the deep intimacy of the God who constantly seeks to bring forth goodness, beauty, and adventure in our lives. God tenderly cared for the Hebraic people, delivering them from captivity, leading them through the wilderness, forgiving their imperfections, and comforting them in exile. God enabled Ruth and Naomi to find new life after the death of their spouses. God gave the cowardly and disloyal followers of Jesus a second chance to become his loyal messengers following Jesus' resurrection. When we cry out, "Where are you when I need you, God?" God responds with authentic love, comfort, and companionship.

2.   *God works for good in all events.*

Progressive Judaism and Christianity affirm that God is neither impotent nor omnipotent but rather a Gentle Force working intimately in our lives and in history to bring forth goodness and beauty. Like a good parent, God relates to a concrete world—a world that is "good," even though it is far from perfect—in terms of God's vision of what it can be. Immanent in all things, God works within all things to bring about relief and transformation. Even in apparently negative events, God is working for good. The Holy One is not the source of illness or violence, but the ground of healing. God frees the captives, heals the sick, and comforts the dying.

God neither causes cancer nor punishes us with AIDS, earthquakes, loss of employment, or tragic events. But God works within these painful events to bring comfort by inspiring friends and relatives, physicians, and nurses, police and rescue workers, by influencing social attitudes, and by presenting the individuals involved with visions that inspire freedom, choice, and creativity.

To say that "in all things God works for good" (Romans 8:28) means that the Holy One is present even in events God does not will as the Gentle Force for healing, wholeness, and reconciliation. God is on our side, whether we have recently divorced, shouted unnecessarily at our children, obsessed over the outcome of an HIV test, or struggled to overcome an addiction. As Harold Kushner, author of *When Bad Things Happen to Good People,* notes, "I don't believe that God causes mental retardation, or chooses who should suffer from muscular dystrophy. The God I believe in does not send us the problem. [God] gives us the strength to cope with the problem."[2]

---

2   Harold Kushner, *When Bad Things Happen to Good People* (New York: Avon, 1981), p. 127.

We believe that the Compassionate One was present in the courage of the firefighters and police who risked their lives to save hundreds in the World Trade Center. We see Divine inspiration in those who sacrificed their lives in order to divert the hijacked plane from a populous area. We experience God's touch in those who comfort the bereaved and in the gradual process of healing of those who mourn loved ones who died at the World Trade Center, the Pentagon, in the Afghan conflict, or in the hospice. God is with us in the light and darkness of our lives as the source of inspiration and the courage to try one more time.

3.   *God feels our pain.*

In his classic account of the Holocaust, *Night*, Eli Wiesel describes the horrific scene of a young boy being hung by the German authorities:

> For more than half an hour he stayed there, struggling between life and death, dying in slow agony under our eyes. And we had to look him full in the face. He was still alive, when I passed in front of him. His tongue was still red, his eyes not yet glazed.
> Behind me, I heard the same man asking: "Where is God now?"
> And I heard a voice within me answer him: "Where is He? Here He is—He is hanging here on this gallows."[3]

On further reflection, Wiesel notes that "Auschwitz was not something that came down ready-made from heaven. It was conceived by men, implemented by men,

---

3   Eli Wiesel, *Night* (New York: Bantam, 1987), p. 62.

staffed by men. And their aim was to destroy not only us but you [God] as well. Ought we not to think of your pain, too? Watching your children suffer at the hands of your other children haven't you also suffered?"[4]

In the biblical tradition, God's messenger is described as "the Suffering Servant." God takes on the pain of the world and transforms it into something of beauty. In the Christian tradition, Isaiah's image of the Suffering Servant is identified with the death of Jesus the Christ on behalf of humankind. As we reflect on the significance of the cross for the Christian understanding of God, we recognize that, for good reasons, many Jews feel ambivalent about the cross of Jesus. They have been blamed as Christ-killers. Throughout the centuries, Jews have been seen as deserving of punishment because their ancestors turned their backs on Jesus of Nazareth. While a few first century Jewish leaders may have participated as accomplices to the Roman crucifixion of Jesus, the majority of first century Jews bore no more blame for the crucifixion than the majority of Americans can be explicitly blamed for wartime atrocities or the cross burnings in rural America.

The cross is neither a form of Divine child abuse in which God must sacrifice God's own child to save the world, nor is the power of the cross restricted to one religious group. Christians understand the incarnation and cross of Jesus as the ultimate example of God's infinite love for the world. Wherever truth, love, and healing are present, God is its source—whether in a laboratory, surgical ward, counseling session, or mosque, temple, or church. The cross of Jesus, the Jewish teacher and healer, reveals God as the "fellow sufferer who understands."[5] God feels the pain of Je-

4 Eli Wiesel, "A Prayer for the Days of Awe," *New York Times* (October 2, 1997), A25.
5 Alfred North Whitehead, *Process and Reality: Corrected Edition* (New York: The Free Press, 1978), p. 351.

sus of Nazareth and God feels our pain. Human choices and Jesus' own willingness to share God's love with his Jewish companions and the whole world brought Jesus to the cross. As Nikos Katzanzakis suggests in *The Last Temptation of Christ,* Jesus could have chosen the quiet life of a rabbi, business person, and family man rather than conflict and suffering. Instead, Jesus chose the path of love for all persons regardless of the consequences.

But for Christians, the death of Jesus is not the end of the story. The peaceable kingdom of the Suffering Servant still inspires humankind to acts of justice and reconciliation. Jesus' dream of healing and wholeness for all persons lives on in the hearts of Christians and non-Christians alike—as in Mahatma Gandhi's vision for non-violence, in Martin Luther King, Jr.'s dream of "the beloved community." While we cannot capture the mystery of the resurrection of Jesus any more than we can fully understand the reality of suffering and pain, the early Christian visions of Christ reveal that God's love is stronger than death. Though God is not all-powerful, God is infinitely resourceful in responding to the evils of the world and our own personal struggles.

The Eternal is with us in our pain and grief as the closest companion, guiding, inspiring, and comforting us at every moment of life. The Holy One is at work even in suffering and evil to bring forth healing and reconciliation. God is inspiring those who suffer to claim their own creativity, to courageously face their pain, and to reach out toward others even in their pain. God patiently brings beauty and growth out of the tragedies of life.

4.   *God invites us to be active partners in transforming suffering.*

Our freedom and our actions matter to God. We can choose life and pattern our lives after Moses, Esther, Jesus, Mohammed, Gandhi, or Mother Teresa. In so doing, we support God's evolving aim at beauty and love. But we can also choose death.

In relationship to God, we are not impotent. We must look at power from a new perspective, the power of Divine parenting that supports growth, freedom, and creativity as it invites us to become partners transforming the universe. Our prayers, spiritual endeavors, and ethical actions make a difference. They create a "field of force" which surrounds us with goodness and beauty and enables God to be more active in the process of personal and social transformation. Our choices and thoughts are the materials that the Divine Artist uses to transform our lives and mend the world. While the impact of the environment and our choices can limit God's presence in our lives, when we align ourselves with the highest good for ourselves and others, God can act in surprising and dramatic ways. Miracles, surprising manifestations of Divine creativity, come from our partnership with the Holy One and our willingness to co-create with God to bring beauty to ourselves, our families, and our world.

Every event arises from the dynamic interplay of three forces: the loving presence of God who influences all things; the moment-by-moment choices we make; and the pervasive influence of our environment, which includes unconscious drives, DNA, family of origin, human choices regarding economics and ecology, nature, accidents, and acts of evil-doers as well as life-givers. God is not powerless within this dynamic matrix of events. In fact, the Holy One is the primary partner in the process of creation and growth, weaving together all the multiple influences in order to ensure the best possible outcome for each and every thing that exists.

This ecological vision of life enables us to reframe the relationship between God and suffering. But, more importantly, it inspires us to discover our true responsibility in facing the personal suffering and the evils we experience as members of the human community. The universe plays dice. Accidents happen, but this is not the whole story! If we look deeply into our experience, we can glimpse a creative interplay of choice, accident, and relationship. Deep down, we may even glimpse the broad and gentle movements of a Force working within the events of our lives that does not coerce us into goodness or punish us for evil but invites us to envisage creative purposes beyond our own self-interest.

We believe that Divine power, human action, and environmental influence are woven together in shaping our total experience. This insight does not solve the mystery of natural disasters or moral evil, but it can help us discover a new partnership with God and a liberating vision of personal and communal freedom when life's challenges threaten to overwhelm us. Beyond impotence and omnipotence lies the vision of a God who loves us so deeply that the Eternal shares in our pain and rejoices in our triumphs. Evil is not God's will nor does the Holy One stand aloof when we suffer. God is always there as our friend when we need comfort and support. The All Loving One helps us discover what we can do to bring forth beauty and meaning from the suffering of life.

5.   *God hears our prayers.*

Physicians and theologians are now studying the power of prayer. While no one can quantify prayer, these studies imply that we live in a non-local universe in which our prayers radiate across the universe without the limitations of space or time. Prayer is an act of love. But prayer also points to the reality a loving and listening God who is on our side. Our prayers point to our faith in God who wants us to have abundant life and joyful relationships.

Emmanuel, God with us, is in the midst of our lives, hearing our prayers and weaving our deepest longings into a fabric of healing that includes everyone.

Our whispered prayers find a listening ear. God hears our sighs. The Holy One knows our hearts from inside out. God is the soul of the universe, the mind of the cosmic body, shaping and being shaped by everything that occurs. This is the true meaning of love: Love actively seeks the well-being of the beloved, but love also listens and allows itself to be changed by the beloved! God and the world exist in creative reciprocity: The Eternal One constantly influences our lives, and we constantly influence God's life and God's ability to shape the world.

Answered and unanswered prayers do not come from the hands of an arbitrary ruler who is absent until we beg for deliverance and mercy. In the matrix of life, God weaves our prayers with environmental and genetic factors, as well as personal choices to help us find a healing of the spirit even when a physical cure or dramatic change is impossible. As the prophet Jeremiah proclaims, "For surely I know the plans I have for you, says the Lord, plans for your welfare and not for harm, to give you a future with hope" (Jeremiah 29:11). The God of Israel and Jesus is merciful.

Finding Angels in Boulders

While we must still ask the question "God, where are you when I need you?" we must also be willing to answer the question "How do I choose life in a world in which death and suffering surround me?"

How can we become God's partners in transforming a world in which absolute safety and security are an illusion, in which a terminal illness, a fatal terrorist attack, or financial ruin can strike at any moment? While the answers to these questions are as unique as each person's spiritual journey, we can make choices that place us on a path of partnership with God and creation, that place us on the side of life regardless of our situation or the actions of others. We can choose love rather than fear even in the most challenging situations. We can become God's partners in mending the small worlds of our personal lives and families and the larger worlds of communities and nations.

1. *Suffering is a call to choice.*

First, we must claim our freedom to change our lives and the world. Although we are neither powerless nor fully in control of the world or our own lives, we can still make a difference wherever we are. In her classic *A Ring of Endless Light,* Madeleine L'Engle records the words of Vicky Austin's grandfather. Although the acute leukemia that will eventually kill him has left him confined to his bed, Vicky's grandfather asserts that there is still one thing he can do: He can pray for the world.

This same affirmation is at the heart of Viktor Frankl's image of human empowerment. Although Frankl faced the evils of the Holocaust, he did not lose faith.

Frankl discovered that the prisoners who experienced the greatest well-being were those who responded creatively even to the dehumanization of the death camps. According to Frankl, a person who has a "why" can endure even the most unbearable "how." In his remembrance of his camp experiences, Frankl notes:

> A man who let himself decline because he could not see any future goal found himself occupied with retrospective thoughts . . . . But in robbing the present of its reality there lay a certain danger. It became easy to overlook the opportunities to make something positive of camp life. Regarding our "provisional" existence as unreal was in itself an important factor in causing persons to lose hold on life; everything in a way became pointless. Such people forgot that often it is just such an exceptionally difficult external situation which gives man the opportunity to grow beyond himself. Instead of taking the camp's difficulties as a test of their inner strength, they did not take their life seriously and despised it as something of no consequence. They preferred to close their eyes and live in the past. Life for such people became meaningless.[6]

Even in the darkest times of imprisonment, Frankl challenged himself to be worthy of his sufferings by remembering that even though he had lost everything he had once loved, he still had a sphere of freedom: the ability to choose his attitude toward the suffering he experienced. Just the

---

6   Viktor E. Frankl, *Man's Search for Meaning* (New York: Pocket Books, 1984), pp. 92-93.

smallest commitment to choosing our attitude toward each circumstance, positive and negative, can transform our lives and change the world.

As chaos theory notes, even the smallest changes, such as a butterfly flapping its wings in one part of the country, can radically alter future events in another part of the country. When Rosa Parks refused to move from her seat on the bus, she unleashed the "butterfly effect" that led to civil rights legislation in the United States. The pain of injustice and racism were real, but that day Rosa Parks chose to be an actor rather than a victim. That is our choice as well when the pain and suffering of the world confront us. Every moment gives us the opportunity to say "yes" to life and to choose to make something beautiful out of even the darkest situations.

When she was diagnosed with cancer, Emily initially gave up hope. She felt her life force ebb away from her. Although she took the chemotherapy treatments her doctor recommended, she saw them merely as something she had to do, a necessary evil that might prolong her life a few months at best. Emily joined a cancer support group because her best friend thought it was a good idea. She didn't want to be there and certainly didn't feel like sharing with other "cancer victims." She went just to go through the motions and get her well-meaning friend off her back.

One week, however, everything changed. For the first time, Emily listened to her companions in the group. Though some of them were worse off than she was, she experienced something unique in their attitudes. None of them saw themselves as a victim of cancer. They complained about their pain and cried over the indignities that accompanied their treatment and hospital visits, but they also saw themselves as making significant choices about their treatment and their futures. Emily was astounded as she heard one of her companions state, "They tell me that the cancer may kill me. But that's not my biggest problem. Since the diagnosis, I realize that each day I have a choice. Will I die on the inside before my body dies? Will I give up hope and shut down my heart, or will I make each day count? Will I love this precious life of mine by loving my husband and children and reaching out to others?"

In that moment, Emily realized that she didn't have to be a victim of cancer or anything else. She decided to research complementary as well as conventional medical treatments. She chose to make small steps that would make all the difference in the world. As she went to the hospital for chemotherapy, she affirmed over and over, "I am choosing to have chemotherapy. I may lose my hair, but the treatment is for good. I want to live as long as possible, and the treatment will help me." Emily chose to be an actor in her own medical and spiritual journey. Her commitment to choose became a way of life. Today, two years later, she states, "I don't know how this will end. But now I know that I can make a difference. I can live each day with purpose and love whether I have one week or forty years. I would never have chosen cancer. But in the midst of cancer, I have a new life. I now know how important it is begin each day with an attitude of love and enter each encounter with the choice to love."

Michael faced a similar challenge when university "downsizing" led to the elimination of a position he had held for nearly two decades. Stunned and angry at the institution's decision and uncertain about his professional future in midlife, Michael was faced with the choice of embracing the unknown future or clinging to the security of the dead past. As one who had written and spoken extensively on living by affirmations and opening to God's possibilities for life, he asked himself, "Will I live by my beliefs and trust God to provide a way toward the future, or will I live by hopelessness and fear?" Michael chose to live by the affirmations of faith and hope. Although he did not deny the challenges of a midlife career change, Michael saw a deeper reality: the Divine possibilities that bring new life even in difficult times. Today, Michael is grateful for the "severe mercy" of downsizing. He is now closer to his wife, happier in his work, more open to friendship and support from others, and is even making more money than he did in his prior position.

We are not a victims. God is working in us through insights, Scriptures, inspirational readings, medication, and the companionship of friends. God wants us to live joyously, and God invites us to say "yes" over and over again to our freedom to choose. Much of the world's evil is not accidental. It arises from human decisions. Human decisions, made over and over in the context of the possibilities of our environment, create a Martin Luther King, Jr. or a Charles Manson, a Mother Teresa or an Osama bin Laden. In our freedom to choose, God is gives us the blessing of empowerment and creativity. In our ability to choose, God calls us to be partners and co-creators.

2. *Suffering is a call to compassion.*

Each of us has a mission that is unique. As individuals, we can't solve the problem of evil and eradicate all the suffering in the world, but we can save that part of the planet that is right in front of us by choosing to live by love. We are the incarnation of Divine love. We are God's voice for love and justice right where we are.

As we seek to be God's partners in healing the suffering of the world, we are guided by Divine compassion. When we choose to be partners with God, we experience the beating of God's heart in our heart and feel God's love in our love. Like the Jewish vision of the Messianic era, the Christian image of the healing Christ, or the compassionate spirit of the Buddhist Bodhisattva, our hearts open to the whole world.

After recovering from serious surgery for a non-malignant tumor, Bruce's son, Matt, chose to reach out to children with cancer. He became a "big brother" for a young boy with leukemia, helping him deal with the transition to adolescence, sharing tears and laughter, and enabling him to have a positive vision of adulthood. Struck by the destruction brought about Hurricane Andrew, another college student, Susan, chose to spend her spring break rebuilding houses with Habitat for Humanity. Horrified by the growing number of hate crimes toward homosexual men in their community, a married couple overcame their homophobia as they joined gay and lesbian support groups and challenged homophobic comments in their church and neighborhood. As they admit, "regardless of how we felt about homosexuality in the beginning, we knew that hate was wrong. We could no longer retreat behind our locked doors when we heard the cries of the victims of hate crimes. We didn't ask how persons become gay, lesbian, or bi-sexual, or judge their behaviors any more than we would those of a heterosexual, we just knew that God called us to love our neighbor and that was enough. Despite losing a few friends as a result of our advocacy for gay and lesbian people, we have found a new community of friends, and we have come to experience God's love right where we are in the faces of persons with AIDS and children whose parents have disowned them. Once we grieved our childlessness, now we have a dozen gay and lesbian young adults who see us as spiritual parents who will never abandon them."

Suffering is a call to compassion. Pain is a call to medication and comfort. God sees imperfection as an opportunity for forgiveness and woundedness as an opportunity for healing. According to an Hebraic legend, the Messiah spends his days sitting wounded among the poor. Though in great pain, the Messiah takes off his bandages one at a time. The Messiah chooses to be a wounded healer, living with the pain of life, rather than choosing a "quick fix," because someone may need him and he wants to be ready when their pain calls to him. In like manner, Jesus did not intellectually solve the problem of evil, but Jesus, as Christians believe, transformed evil by love and forgiveness and the unexpected resurrection that reflects God's victory over death and destruction.

Compassion is the gift of stature and imagination. The New Testament says that Jesus grew in wisdom and stature and favor with God and humankind (Luke 2:52). Stature involves our ability to embrace the totality of our experience in all its contradictions and complexity. Evil and suffering are real and can never be denied, but they exist in a broader context that includes adventure, growth, and love. A person of stature embraces the pain and evil of the world, along with her or his own pain and suffering, and integrates it with feelings of hope and trust as well as love and compassion.

The gift of stature enables us to see our imperfections and failures in a larger perspective. The person of stature remembers that there is always "more" to him or herself than the immediate moment of pain and suffering. Pushing ourselves beyond the finite and self-absorbed ego, we identify our well-being with the health of the totality. Death is part of life. Without death, new generations could not emerge and the ecosystem would eventually collapse. Pain and suffering often constrict our experience, but we may choose to transcend our pain and suffering by reaching out to others, and by discovering our particular mission for this time of personal challenge.

3.   *Suffering is a call to imagination.*
     The story is told of the sculptor Michelangelo who was observed by his neighbor hammering on a rough hewn boulder. "Why are you hammering on this boulder his neighbor asked?" To which the sculptor replied, "There's an angel inside, and I'm trying to let it out."
     There is no greater boulder than the experience of pain, bereavement, suffering, and disability. The edges are so jagged and the surface so dense that we can barely see beyond the pain. But if the God of compassion and possibility is our companion, then there is always an angel ready to spring forth. The boulder is real and the pain cannot be denied. Our depression and fear are authentic and cannot be explained away merely as the result of negative thinking. But, in the concreteness of life's boulders, new adventures can emerge.
     The great Christian leader of the first century, Paul of Tarsus, suffered from a chronic illness that would not go away. Time after time, he prayed for deliverance. Even mystical experiences could not free him from this daily torture. But, in the midst of the pain, he heard voice of God, "My grace is sufficient for you, for power is made sufficient in weakness" (2 Corinthians 12:9). The apostle Paul later wrote, "In all things we are more than conquerors through [God] who loved us. For I am convinced that neither death nor life . . . nor anything else in all creation, will be able to

separate us from the love of God" (Romans 8:37-38). In his weakness, Paul discovered strength and the courage to continue on even in the face of tremendous physical and emotional suffering.

"Angels" often appear when least expected. Nathan discovered an angel in the boulder of pancreatic cancer. Successful in business, but impoverished in relationships, the diagnosis of cancer forced Nathan to look at his values from a new perspective. He realized that while he was on his way to the top, his spiritual life was going downhill. Now, his money and power could not save him. He knew he had just a few months at the most to reach out—to his wife, his children, and to God. Not knowing where to start, he simply asked for Divine guidance: "God, help me find my way. God, show me what I need to do with the rest of my life." Though he did not become a new person overnight, Nathan began to see beyond the boulders of his life—his distance from his wife and family and his illness. First, he saw himself with new eyes, not just as a successful business person but as someone capable of sharing love regardless of his physical condition. Then, he saw unexpected beauty and compassion in his wife of thirty years and his grown children. He cracked the boulder of hard-heartedness as he asked each one for forgiveness. Now he could begin anew. While Nathan knew he could not recover the lost years with his wife and children, he could live in an eternal now in which love and compassion were the realities. Even though he was dying, he could choose life and become a partner in God's healing adventure. In his final days, Nathan mourned that it took the diagnosis of cancer to wake him up to love, but he rejoiced that in the darkest night, he found God and a love that healed his spirit. Though Nathan was not cured, his prayer for new life and greater love was answered.

We need to recognize, however, that not all suffering is redemptive. Some people experience long-term pain of body, mind, and spirit with virtually no hope of personal growth, physical relief, or financial recovery. The tears of grief for the spouse who died on September 11th seem endless. Their hope is simply to get through the day or to die in comfort. We can neither minimize nor explain away another's suffering or the spiritual and emotional impact that arises from tragic events such as accidents and terrorist acts. Nor can we blame those who seem to be captured in unending cycles of depression, negativity, and self-destruction. Suffering is a call to love and compassion, not judgment. Sometimes there can be a healing even when there is no cure, and that is simply the gift of endurance and hope that enables us to look beyond the pain of this lifetime even as we face realistically the suffering of the present moment. Our parents in the faith knew that the only way to deal with suffering was to face it and journey through the valley of the shadow of death with God as our companion. In the darkest times we can still find comfort and hope in the presence of the Fellow Sufferer who understands. In such moments, the Psalmist reminds us:

> Where can I go from your spirit? Or where can I flee from your presence? If I ascend to heaven, you are there. . . . If I take the wings of the morning and settle at the farthest limits of the sea, even there your hand shall lead me, and your right hand shall hold me fast. If I say, "Surely the darkness shall cover me, and the light around me become night," even the darkness is not dark to you; the night is as bright as the day, for darkness is as light to you. (Psalm 139:7-12)

Regardless of the circumstances of life in which we find ourselves, God's Shalom embraces and guides us through all things. Even when there is little hope of recovery of health or reconciliation in a relationship, we are not alone. We dwell in God's light and love. In our suffering, God is with us, bringing forth angels from the boulders of our lives.

CHAPTER THREE

Spiritual Resources for Challenging Times

OUR primary task in life is to bring forth angels from the boulders of our lives and the broken world in which we live. In the Hebraic tradition, this process is called *tikkun olam,* or "mending the world." God aspires for us to be "angels," messengers of healing and wholeness. Yet, most of us fail to see the angels hidden within the challenges of life. We see the imperfections, defects, and drawbacks, not the imprints of the Holy Adventure. Like Rip Van Winkle, we need to wake up to the revolutionary potential in and around us. Like the lion raised among goats, we need to see ourselves in the mirror of life and discover that we are meant for beauty, love, strength, creativity, and abundance.

God is constantly opening us to new alternatives, giving us a vision of what we can become when we awaken to our own inner and outer gifts. In the biblical tradition, when the prophet Jeremiah protested that he was too young to speak for God, God challenged him, "Before I formed you

in the womb I knew you, and before you were born I consecrated you . . . Do not say 'I am only a boy'; for you shall go
to all to whom I will send you, and you shall speak whatever
I command you. Do not be afraid of them, for I am with you
to deliver you" (Jeremiah 1:5-8) . When the newly-crowned
Queen Esther pondered her role in saving the Jewish people
from persecution, her mentor Mordecai challenged her to
claim her place in history with the words, "Who knows?
Perhaps you have come to royal dignity for just such a time
as this" (Esther 4:14). In that same spirit, the Christian tradition believes that Jesus of Nazareth fully expressed the
Divine potential that is available to all of us. Each moment
he actualized God's vision for his life and saw the Divine vision for everyone he met. He saw deep love and devotion in
prostitutes. He brought forth courage from the faltering and
cowardly Peter. He imagined wholeness and healing when
others saw failure and disability. When his disciples obsessed on how they would feed five thousand with a few
loaves and fishes, Jesus saw God's abundant care bursting
forth to feed the hungry and thirsty, not only on the hillside
in Israel but in countless villages across the globe. From five
loaves and two fish, a whole multitude could be fed. Jesus
affirmed his calling as the messenger of Divine wholeness
and transformation, the embodiment of the prophets'
dream of Shalom.

The prophetic vision embodied in Jesus and in the
Hebrew sages invites us to experience that same Shalom in
our own lives. God sees the potential for spiritual greatness
in us. We are meant for abundant life. We are meant to
change the world. But to claim our partnership with God,
we need to claim our spiritual resources. We need to inten-
tionally awaken ourselves to God's empowering presence in
our lives.

Our "Top Ten" Spiritual Resources

The ability to respond creatively to suffering, adversity, and conflict results from the interplay of a life-supporting vision of God and the cultivation of spiritual resources that enable us to remain calm and centered amid the storms of life. While there are many aspects of spiritual nurture and sustenance to consider, we have chosen to highlight ten inner resources that are available to each one of us, regardless of our circumstances.

1.   Self-esteem

Perhaps the most basic resource we have is the experience of personal significance and self-esteem. People with self-esteem can face the moral, environmental, and spiritual challenges of life with confidence in their ability to remain steadfast, centered, and strong.

To children who see their future in terms of failure, poverty, drug addiction, and unwed pregnancy, minister and politician Jesse Jackson leads the chant "I am somebody!" Hope for personal growth and social change comes from recognizing that we are not limited by economics, physical condition, age, gender, or previous life history. In each moment, we are free to choose a new path and claim a new future.

Yet, self-esteem is a challenge for many of us. Just look at the prophet Isaiah. When he encountered God at the Jerusalem Temple, he hid his face and cried in terror, "Woe is me! I am lost." The Eternal One didn't accept his fear or imperfection as the final word. God sent an angel to cleanse his tongue and awaken his spirit, and then asked, "Whom shall I send, and who will go for us?" Emboldened by the spirit of self-esteem, Isaiah responded, "Here am I; send me!" (Isaiah 6:5,8).

When Moses encountered the Holy One clothed in a burning bush, he wanted to run away (Exodus 3-4). He protested that his inability to speak publicly rendered him unworthy to lead his people from slavery to freedom. "Let someone else more qualified go to Pharaoh," Moses cried. "Choose someone like my brother, Aaron, to challenge Pharaoh's injustice." But God saw a national hero in this retiring and tongue-tied shepherd with an ambiguous past.

God always sees more in us than we see in ourselves. Sometimes we need to stop and ask ourselves, "What am I missing about myself that God sees so clearly in me?"

The issue of self-esteem was central to Martin Luther's role in the Protestant Reformation. Traumatized by a distant, demanding, and judging father, young Luther never felt he was good enough for the Holy One. Although he entered the monastery to escape his fears of damnation and eventually rose to the top of the academic world, Luther still felt guilt and anxiety whenever he pondered his relationship with God. In his eyes, there was an infinite distance between holy God and sinful humankind. The Supreme Sovereign was perfect, but Luther saw himself as a worm, unworthy of anything but hell-fire and brimstone. Burdened by his guilt, Luther obsessively confessed his sinfulness each day until his confessor, in frustration, confronted him, "Don't come back for confession until you do something serious like murder, adultery, or theft." Luther found his freedom when he could accept that the Holy One loved him fully despite all his imperfection.

In discovering God's intimate love, Luther also discovered his own value as a child of God—and the courage to protest against the moral corruption of church leaders in Rome. Even when he found himself tormented by fear and depression and always struggling with claiming the image of a loving God, Luther experienced solace as he scribbled the affirmation on his desk, "I was baptized," which reminded Luther that he was in God's hands forever. Regardless of how he felt about himself, Luther knew that he belonged to God and that the Divine love would sustain him. Luther discovered amid his own anxiety and fear that he was "somebody." He found the angel of love and grace in life's boulders and changed the world. His spiritual journey became a testimony of God's loving care to countless others throughout the centuries. Luther became a lion and he roared!

Self-esteem is the gift of a transformed vision of ourselves and our potential, grounded in our relationship to the Creator of love and beauty (Genesis 1:26-28). As Genesis proclaims, we are created, male and female, in God's image. The Divine imprint is our deepest reality. We bear the reflection of God in every thought, word, and deed. Each of us, as Ralph Waldo Emerson affirmed, is "a bard of the Holy Spirit," a messenger of Divine love and creativity to the world. We are loved by an infinite Spirit who calls us by name and gives us a task that no one else in the universe can duplicate. We are unique in the whole universe. Without each of our particular gifts, the universe remains incomplete and imperfect.

The gift of self-esteem transformed Doug's life. The son of a world-famous scientist, Doug felt he would never measure up to his father's success, notoriety, or intelligence. Though he tried to follow in his father's footsteps, he failed miserably. He dropped out of graduate school and settled for a lucrative, yet humdrum, career as a civil servant. His low self-esteem spilled over into his marriage and family life. His wife's professional accomplishments threatened his sense of worth, but he alternated between anger and withdrawal in relation to her. Deep down, he knew that his life was hollow. Without a change of heart, he would lose everything he loved. At his thirtieth high school reunion, Doug synchronously found himself sitting next to a former basketball teammate. When his classmate told of his spiritual adventures and journey to wholeness, Doug realized that he could change his life, too, and that his best years truly lay ahead of him.

Doug's transformation was difficult. He had to see himself from a new perspective. Doug began constantly reminding himself that he was a child of God, created in the Divine image. He knew he needed to break old thought patterns and behaviors to claim this new self. For a while he wasn't sure who he was, as he began to let go of his life-long sense of failure. He asked his wife's forgiveness and committed himself to supporting her career. He learned to honor her accomplishments as being as important as his own. But, more importantly, he began to see himself in a new light. He learned to look beyond what he assumed to be failure to see what was truly good about himself: his love for his children, his professional skills, his service to the community—and his willingness to change. He saw that his sense of failure arose from his attempt to be someone other than his deepest self. Doug realized that the only person he needed to measure up to was the person God intended him to be.

Today, Doug is proud of his accomplishments as a public servant and recognizes that his commitment to excellence has made a difference to thousands of lower income residents of his county. He and his wife enjoy a new partnership in mutual self-affirmation, even as they rejoice in their grown children's accomplishments.

Now, Doug judges his life by his own personal version of the Jewish proverb, originally told by Rabbi Zusia:

"When the Messiah comes, he will not ask if you were David or Moses, but were you Doug? Did you become the person you were meant to be?" Doug found an angel in the boulder of low self-esteem, and now he knows that when the Messiah questions him, he will confidently respond, "Yes, I am Doug, and I lived fully, as God's spirit called me to live."

2.   *Self-image*

Our self-esteem is physical as well as spiritual in nature. Many of us lose confidence in ourselves because we imagine ourselves failing to measure up to an image of perfect physical well-being. Authentic self-affirmation honors our present state of physical, emotional, and spiritual life, even as it challenges us to aim at greater fitness and well-being.

"Your body is a temple of the Holy Spirit," asserted the early Christians (1 Corinthians 6:19). They believed that God of Israel was so concerned with the world of bodies and relationships that God became flesh in Jesus of Nazareth to bring wholeness to every aspect of life. Jesus' first miracle was turning water into wine at a marriage feast and, thus, blessing the intimacy of marriage and sexuality and the joy of celebration. These first century Christians were affirming the insights of their Jewish mothers and fathers who proclaimed that God created the physical world, sexuality, family life, and relationships to be "very good" (Genesis 1:1-31). The Holy One created a world bathed in beauty. "The heavens are telling the glory of God," (Psalm 19:1) and so do the everyday functions of digestion, circulation, and sexuality. One of the great events of Israel's history is the birth of the legendary Isaac to the aged and barren couple, Abraham and Sarah. Centuries later, God responded to

Hannah's prayer for a child. From childless parents, a boy Samuel was born, who was to become one of the first spiritual leaders of Israel (1 Samuel 1-2). Puritans beware! God is interested in healthy sexuality. God wants us to flourish in the world of the flesh.

The universe, intimately revealed in the unity of mind and body, is the primary revelation of God. But many of us are uneasy with this Divine revelation when it comes to our bodies. For many of us, the body is anything *but* a beloved manifestation of Divine creativity. Our body is the ultimate boulder, jagged, misshapen, abused, emaciated, disabled, or overweight. We see the aging process as an enemy and a sign that we are no longer desirable. We constantly compare our bodies to the perfectly sculpted frames of movie stars and supermodels. Even though the basic guidelines for physical wholeness are simple and straightforward—healthy diet, exercise, rest and meditation, abstinence from tobacco, moderate drinking—we continue to mistreat our bodies day after day.

Steve hated his body. When he looked into the mirror, he hated everything about himself. He could see nothing attractive about his forty-inch waist, receding hairline, red hair, and freckled face. In his eyes, everyone was healthier, happier, and more handsome. "With a body like this, who will ever love me?" he asked himself. "I can't even stand looking at myself." But one morning everything changed. As he looked in the mirror at his thirty-something, robust physique, he remembered a passage he had read recently in Genesis: "God created humankind in [the Divine] image" (Genesis 1:26-27).

While Steve didn't think of God as a physical being, he realized that this Scripture said that God created *him*—body, mind, and spirit—and though he might need to spend more time on his physical and spiritual well-being, he was good just as he was. For the first time in his life, Steve realized that the Eternal One loved and accepted him, whether he was slender or rotund. He didn't need to be a hunk in order to be healthy, happy, or loved. Steve realized that he needed to love himself in light of the love God had for him.

Following this spiritual epiphany, Steve made a choice to love his body, and his self-acceptance led to action. He began an exercise program involving swimming and walking. He reduced his consumption of sugar, red meat, and alcohol. He began a daily practice of meditative prayer. Each day he looked in the mirror and affirmed, "I am created in God's image. I am healthy and whole just as I am." Steve's life was transformed. Recently, this life-long couch potato ran six miles in the Susan B. Komen Race for the Cure to honor two co-workers who had survived breast cancer. Though he still is a few pounds overweight and his hair line has receded a bit more, Steve now thanks God when he looks in the mirror. He's happy with the person on the outside, but more than that, he loves the person on the inside. His growing affirmation of his self-image, and its impact on his self-esteem, is reflected in his recent engagement and plans for marriage in the upcoming year.

Affirming that our body is the temple of God involves recognizing the Divine presence in our bodies. Whether we are culturally beautiful and young, aging, or experiencing a chronic illness or disability, our bodies are a unique manifestation of Divine artistry. In spite of cultural stereotypes, there is no *one* perfect body. Indeed, as beloved children of God, our bodies are whole and complete just as they are.

Jane affirms her body each day with the words, "I

thank you, God, for my beautiful body. I thank you for life and the ability to affirm others. Help me to see your beauty in myself and in everyone I meet." Though she must navigate the world with a wheelchair, Jane loves God in the world of the flesh, her own flesh. She has discovered angels within where others see boulders, and she has become a gentle artist of the spirit enabling others to see the holy in their own injured bodies. Her spiritual wholeness enables her to live fully and transcend the disabilities others see in her physical body. "Just as I am, I am healthy and whole, and I share my wholeness with everyone I meet," Jane explains. With Jane, we can claim the unique wholeness of our body, mind, and spirit that inspires us to seek well-being in every aspect of our lives.

3.   *Self-confidence*

Each one of us is a singularity. In the words of the Christian teacher Paul of Tarsus, each of us has an unrepeatable role in the "body of Christ" (2 Corinthians 12). While envy and insecurity constantly tempt us to judge our value in comparison to others, self-confidence invites us to treasure and develop our particular gifts as a means of contributing to the well-being of all things.

Traditionally, persons of faith have seen the discovery of our unique vocation or calling as one of life's goals. Like Esther, we are called to discover our unique gifts for mending the world in "just such a time as this." Within the "body of Christ," each of us has an essential place.

Perhaps this is the reason many of us watch the Jimmy Stewart movie *It's a Wonderful Life* each December. It is a vivid testimony to the importance of a single life. Sunk in despair at his economic misfortunes, George Bailey wishes he hadn't been born. But his depression lifts when his angelic visitor reveals how significant his life has been. Without his unique existence, his brother, who was to become a war hero, would have died; a beautiful young woman would not have experienced love; a pharmacist would have poisoned a patient; and his hometown would have been a place of poverty rather than hope.

For many people, self-confidence requires transcending the voices of oppression and negativity. That spirit of transformation was embodied in the courage and strength of Nelson Mandela and Bishop Desmond Tutu in South Africa, both of whom soared above others' definitions of their worth. Apartheid is a heresy, Tutu asserted, because it denies the image of God in persons of color. Regardless of what others may think, we are all children of God, endowed with infinite worth, and deserving of infinite respect.

Having self-confidence means believing we can make a difference in the world. It means trusting that, regardless of the environment or our past, we can take a step toward creativity, love, and freedom.

Self-confidence emerges when we recognize that we are partners in God's creation of the world. When the prophet Jeremiah protested his youth, God proclaimed that Jeremiah was called from the womb and that God would always be with him. When the prophet Isaiah bemoaned his failures, God challenged him to go beyond his limits by giving him even greater chances. Though she was a humble young woman, Mary of Nazareth said "yes" to the angelic message that her child would reveal God's love and justice to humankind.

Progressive Christianity and Judaism assert that God wants us to achieve the abundant life that is our destiny. God wants us to aim high, as Rabbi Naftali Tavi Horowitz of Ropshitz, the Ropshitzer Rebbe, who lived from 1760-1827, reminds us in this tale:

> During the siege of Sebastopol, Czar Nicholas I was once riding along one of the walls when an enemy archer took aim at him. A Russian soldier who observed this from far off screamed and startled the Czar's horse so it swerved to the side and saved the Czar from certain death.
>
> When the Czar told the soldier to ask for any favor he wanted, the soldier responded, "Our sergeant is so brutal. He is always beating me. If only I could serve under another sergeant, I would be happy."
>
> "Fool," cried Czar Nicholas, "be a sergeant yourself."

The Ropshitzer Rebbe concluded, "We are like that; we pray for the petty needs of the hour and do not know how to pray for the redemption that will change our lives."[7]

There is no need for false humility in our spiritual journeys. Self-confidence helps us to claim the destiny that God has planned for us. Embracing our vocation as God's children inspires us to support the spiritual growth and personal success of others. To paraphrase the words of Jesus of Nazareth in the first person, we can affirm: "I am the light of the world and I will let my light shine, so others can see their light as well" (Matthew 5:14-16).

---

7 Adapted from Martin Buber, *Tales of the Hasidim: The Later Masters*, translated by Olga Marx (New York: Schocken, 1948), p. 194.

4.   *Courage*

Ordinary people do extraordinary things when they discover that their lives can truly make a difference. When they boarded the plane on September 11, 2001, the passengers of Flight 93 did not expect to be heroes. But when they learned that their hijackers intended to use their airplane as a weapon of terror, they sprang into action. Though they lost their lives, they may have prevented the destruction of the Capitol or the White House and the death of thousands. Like countless persons before them, they sacrificed their lives for a greater good. They discovered a larger sense of self in which their well-being was intimately connected with the well-being of people they would never meet. Faced with a life-and-death challenge, they summoned the strength of spirit to face fear and pain with the affirmation, "Let's roll!"

The biblical tradition tells the story of three ordinary yet courageous people, Shadrach, Meshach, and Abednego (Daniel 3:1-30). When the Babylonian king Nebuchadnezzar ordered all his subjects to worship a golden statue, these three Jewish civil servants refused to bow down. Enraged the king threatened them: "If you do not worship the god I have made, I will throw you into a flaming furnace." Still, Shadrach, Meshach, and Abednego chose to follow the God of Israel. The king raised the temperature of the furnace to such a degree that the men who carried the prisoners to the furnace perished from its heat. But as he gazed into the furnace, the king was shocked. Instead of three men, he saw four persons, and one of them looked like a god. These ordinary men became heroes when they found God in the midst of an inferno.

Centuries later, the Gospels tell of a woman who had been burdened with a flow of blood for twelve years.

Despite the pain of her chronic illness, her role as a woman in a patriarchal society, and the social ostracism she faced from an illness that rendered her ritually unclean, she dared to touch Jesus. She believed that God would respond to her faith and make her whole once again. Her faith led to courage and the healing she sought (Mark 5:26-34).

For many of us, the greatest test of courage is our willingness to affirm our personal integrity in the midst of conflict and challenge. Dominated by fear and anxiety, or tempted by personal gain, too often we follow the path of least resistance and lose our spiritual center. We turn our back on our values, moral commitments, and faith. We betray our spouses, friends, ourselves, and God. Yet, the moment we remember that we are rooted in God and that our lives reflect God's presence, we gain our bearings once more. We can face conflict, ridicule, and failure, knowing that honesty, fidelity, love, and justice are more important than success or even survival.

Courage empowers us to leave a toxic relationship, speak up for what we believe, quit a job we hate, ask for forgiveness, heal a broken marriage, or open ourselves to love, even though we've been hurt before. Courage inspires us to ask for what we truly need in a job, a relationship, or a business deal. Courage enables us to face an uncertain future after the death of a loved one, a divorce, a serious illness, or the loss of a job. When we act with courage, even in small things, we also affirm that our needs and personal integrity are important. In the words of Hillel, "If I am not for myself, who will be."

A Hasidic tale notes that, once upon a time, Rabbi Elimelech's servant forgot a spoon for Rabbi Mendel, who was a guest at Rabbi Elimelech's table. Everyone ate except Rabbi Mendel. When Rabbi Elimelech asked, "Why aren't

you eating," his guest replied, "I have no spoon." In response, Rabbi Elimelech asserted, "Look, you must know
enough to ask for a spoon, and a plate too, if need be!" Rabbi
Mendel took the word of his teacher to heart. From that day
on, his fortunes improved.[8]

It has been said that courage is fear that has said its
prayers. The heroic person is not fearless, but faces fear with
confidence in God's trustworthiness. When God called Moses to ask Pharaoh to liberate the children of Israel from
bondage, he protested his limitations and handicaps. The
task seemed larger to Moses than his own abilities. But God
responded to his protest, "I will be with you" (Exodus
3:12). Armed with Divine companionship, Moses cast off
his timidity and low self-esteem and became a lion of liberation. Years later, when the Jewish people sought to enter Israel, they were overwhelmed by the size and strength of the
inhabitants. "When we compare ourselves to them, we feel
like grasshoppers standing before giants," they stammered
in fear. The people gained courage when they heard God's
assurance, "Be strong and courageous; do not be frightened
or dismayed, for the Lord your God is with you wherever you
go" (Joshua 1:9). Centuries later, the Christian tradition affirms this same assurance in the words "do not be afraid"
that empowered the perplexed young Mary and her confused
fiancé, Joseph, to become the parents of Jesus the Savior.

Courage arises from the gift of faith. While faith involves the vision of God as our companion and anchor in all
of life's challenges, faith is also, as Martin Luther proclaimed, "a lively, reckless confidence in the grace of God."
In spite of our fear, imperfection, and doubt, we trust that

8 Buber, *Tales of the Hasidim*, p. 125.

God is with us, giving us exactly what we need to respond creatively and courageously to the internal and external challenges we face.

Just as the pioneers of our faith, Abraham and Sarah set off to an unknown land, trusting that God would be their guide and companion each step of the way, we, too, are called to journey to new and unknown places of mind, body, spirit, and relationships. Our future is open and our actions truly matter.

5.   *Faith*

One day, Jesus and his disciples set off on sailing trip across the Sea of Galilee. As the disciples enjoyed the beautiful day, Jesus went to sleep in the bow of the boat. Suddenly, a storm broke all around them. The sky turned dark, thunder crashed, and waves pummeled their small craft. In panic, the disciples feared for their lives until they remembered that Jesus was in the boat with them. In that moment, their fear subsided and they knew that they would be safe. They awakened Jesus who then calmed the sea. The storm still raged, but their hearts were at peace, for they knew that they were in God's hands. As they sailed toward shore, once again in sunshine, Jesus asked his disciples, "Where is your faith?" (Luke 8:25).

Today many people describe the constantly shifting nature of life as "perpetual white water." Amid the challenges of our world, daily stress may become distress of mind, body, or spirit. We may find ourselves on high alert, dominated by the "fight or flight response." Eventually our distress may manifest itself in high blood pressure, recurring colds, and the onset of more serious diseases.

Although the author of Psalm 46 lived in an agrarian society, he nevertheless experienced the radical uncertainty of human life. The Hebraic author noted that external and internal tumult can overwhelm even the bravest soul: the mountains falling into the sea, the waves crashing against the shore, war at the gates of the city. Still, amid this spiritual tsunami, the author counseled, "Be still, and know that I am God! . . . The God of Jacob is our refuge" (Psalm 46:10-11). Peace of mind is the gift of knowing that we are always in God's hands. For those who find the Divine Center, there is a still point in the tumult of life, peace amid the storm.

Martin Luther King, Jr., discovered this peace amid the storms of racism and hatred. In his sermon "Our God is Able," King related his own experience of discovering the peace of God in perilous times.[9] One evening during the most contentious days of the Montgomery, Alabama, bus boycott, King received an anonymous phone call that threatened the lives of his family and himself. Trembling with fear and unable to sleep, King went downstairs to make a cup of coffee. As the coffee brewed, King bowed his head at the kitchen table and prayed aloud, confessing his fear and asking for guidance.

In that moment of despair, King experienced the peace of God in a way that would change his life. King heard the quiet, yet powerful assurance of inner spiritual guidance and empowerment. He knew that if he took the path of righteousness, God would be his companion forever. No longer uncertain of his calling, King was ready to face anything. Though the outer situation of violence, injustice, and threat remained, King felt an inner calm that came from God's presence.

9 Martin Luther King, *Strength to Love* (Philadelphia: Fortress Press, 1963), pp. 113-114.

In the years ahead, King lived by the inner calm that God gave him as he faced beatings and imprisonment. Even as he pondered the possibility of an early death, King still had a dream. Though he might not make it to the promised land, King knew that God was faithful, and that justice and love would triumph over evil and hatred. King knew what it meant to have peace amid the storm.

It has been said that there are only two kinds of people in the world: those who are in God's hands and know it, and those who are in God's hands and don't know it. Faith reminds us that we are always in the caring hands of the Eternal, and that the Holy One is giving us everything we need to face the challenges of today and tomorrow regardless of the current situation of our lives.

The peace that comes from knowing that we are in God's hands is the gift of "basic trust" that eludes so many of us in childhood. Even though we may fear the future, we can trust the promise of God that the Holy One will be our companion, protector, and source of courage and creativity even in the most challenging situations.

6.   Hope

Some of life's most basic questions involve our attitude toward the future: Is the future trustworthy? Are we doomed to repeat the past or can we boldly begin a new life? Can we shape a new future? Do we believe that we can bring forth angels out of life's boulders?

Hope arises from trusting that the future is in the care of a dynamic God who constantly awakens and empowers us to be partners in a Holy Adventure. Progressive Jews and Christians see God as the Gentle Force who moves through all things, urging us forward, challenging us with new possibilities, and inspiring us to restless adventure.

This Holy Adventure reminds us, moment by moment, that we can freely change our lives and make a difference to others. As partners in God's adventure of abundant life, we have the freedom to change even the most difficult present in light of the Holy Future that awaits us. When we perceive the world in terms of surprise and novelty, the future is always open, and we can always claim new life. Synchronous meetings and serendipitous encounters await us around every corner. In every limitation, there is an angel of possibility and growth ready to spring forth.

Rabbi Nachman of Breslov told the following story as a reminder that, because we never know how things will turn out, we should never give up hope. Once upon a time, a poor man named Moshe earned his living by digging and selling clay. One day while digging in the clay, he discovered a precious stone. When he took the stone to the local jeweler, the jeweler told him, "This stone is so valuable, no one here can afford such a stone. Go to London, and there you will be able to sell it." Moshe was so poor that he could not even afford to make the journey to the seacoast. He sold everything he had and went from house to house, begging for money for the trip.

When he finally arrived at the seacoast, Moshe showed his stone to a sea captain, who immediately gave him a first-class cabin and treated him as if he were wealthy. One day, however, Moshe forgot to put his stone in a safe place. As he napped after his noon meal, the ship steward cleared the table where Moshe had left the stone, shaking both the crumbs and the stone into the sea. When he awakened and realized what had happened, Moshe initially panicked. He knew that the captain was ruthless and would not hesitate to kill him if he were unable to pay his bill. Having no other choice, Moshe continued to act as if he still possessed the stone.

One day, the captain said to him, "I want to buy a large quantity of wheat and sell it in London for a huge profit. But if I buy it in my own name, I am afraid that I will be accused of stealing from the king's treasury. Therefore, I will arrange for it to be bought in your name, and I will pay you well for your trouble." Having nothing to lose, Moshe agreed. But as soon as they arrived in London, the sea captain died, leaving Moshe the entire shipload of wheat. When he returned home, a wealthy man, his neighbors saw that he was joyful as ever. His joy infected everyone he met. Rabbi Nachman concluded, "The diamond did not belong to Moshe, and the proof is that he did not keep it. The wheat, however, did belong to him, and the proof is that he kept it. But he got what he deserved only because he remained happy." [10]

Hope is the open door to the future. Our hopefulness not only shapes our experience of the world and opens us to creative responses in difficult situations, it can also change the world. Hope is like the "butterfly effect"—where a butterfly fluttering its wings in California can significantly alter the weather in faraway New York City. The smallest decisions can awaken us to Divine possibility. We can shape the world precisely because we live in a world characterized by interrelatedness and mutual empowerment.

Small changes can make all the difference. In the midst of a crisis in their marriage, Bruce and Kate Epperly discovered a hopeful future for their relationship simply by changing the way they viewed each other. Instead of looking at what was lacking in their marriage and each other, they chose to focus on the angels within the boulders of them-

---

10 Adapted from *Rabbi Nachman's Stories,* translated by Aryeh Kaplan (Brooklyn: Breslov Research Institute, 1983), pp. 467-468.

selves and their relationship. Inspired by psychiatrist Jerry Jampolsky's work in attitudinal healing, they chose to look at the light and not the lampshade, to become "love finders" rather than "fault finders."[11] In committing themselves to see differently and to treat each other with grace and dignity, this once-troubled couple found their marriage renewed and revitalized. Despite the dire prognostications of one marriage counselor, Bruce and Kate chose to affirm the deeper reality of God's presence and their own inner resources for healing and transformation. In claiming the wholeness of their lives, including the places of pain and conflict, they discovered the angels in each other and in the problems they faced.

A hopeful and optimistic attitude can make the difference between life and death. Over the years, physicians O. Carl Simonton and Bernie Siegel have noticed that hopelessness, passivity, and inability to contemplate the possibility of change are often associated with the onset of cancer. In contrast, people with life-threatening illnesses enhance their likelihood of survival from cancer and other serious illnesses when they commit themselves to personal transformation. In the intricate relationship of mind, body, and emotions, our beliefs influence our physiology. Optimism and hope can stimulate the life-supporting processes of the immune system. Even if they do not receive a physical cure, patients with hope experience a healing that embraces the totality of their lives and enables them to live with confidence, compassion, and hope even at their death beds.

---

11 Jerry Jampolsky, *Love is Letting Go of Fear* (Milbrae, CA; Celestial Arts, 1979); and Susan Trout, *To See Differently* (Washington D.C.: Three Roses Press, 1990). For a description of their process of marriage transformation, see Bruce Epperly, *The Power of Affirmative Faith: A Spirituality of Personal Transformation* (St. Louis: Chalice Press, 2001).

A hopeful attitude recognizes that, although pain and suffering are real, they are not the *only* reality. Hope liberates us from the prison of negativity precisely because it gives us the courage to explore new frontiers of possibility.

The story is told of the night of the falling stars. One evening there was a meteor shower, and the residents of a small African village panicked at the sight. They were sure that the world was coming to an end. They rushed from one side of the forest to the other shouting, "The sky is falling. The end is near." Worn out by their panic, they finally sought the guidance of the wise woman of the village. As she gazed contemplatively at the stars, she reflected on the heavenly tumult: "Yes, look at all the stars that are falling. But look more carefully. See all the stars that are still and constant."

Many of us of live apocalyptically. We go from one crisis to the next. Each event takes on cosmic proportions as it threatens to destroy our world. We constantly take the temperature of our relationships, our jobs, and our children's well-being. We fixate on the negative signs of the times. We live as if chaos were king, and beauty and order had no enduring value.

Yes, cancer and racism exist. And we must never forget the Holocaust or the terrorist acts of September 11th. And, of course the evening news continues to announce terrorist attacks, toxic spills, governmental and corporate misconduct, failing schools, traffic gridlock, violence in the streets as if they were the only reality. But there is a deeper reality that lies beneath the headlines. Hope arises from the vision that we are part of a Holy Adventure, guided by the love of God. This larger vision of reality puts our lives in perspective and gives us the courage and patience to change the world.

In the award-winning film *Life is Beautiful,* a father and son are imprisoned during the Holocaust. Recognizing that if his son is discovered by the Nazi guards, the boy will be sent to the gas chamber, the father creates an alternative reality, an interactive game for his son in which the boy is rewarded for creatively facing the hardships of the concentration camp. To his fellow prisoners, the father's game appears to be pure foolishness, even though they go along with it, but the father's imagination enables his son to evade detection by the prison guards. When it comes down to it, we must ask, "Which is more real: the diabolical indignities of the concentration camp or the father's loving imagination?"

Biblical scholar Walter Brueggemann notes that one of the primary characteristics of the Hebrew prophets was the ability to imagine an alternative reality to the present dismal and dehumanizing state of affairs. When illness or tragedy strikes, we are challenged to become twenty-first century prophets, who imagine our body's immune system flushing out cancer cells, who take stands against racism and injustice, who claim a new career after an unexpected corporate collapse, who confront terrorists on an airplane, who stand in our truth as we seek to heal our relationships with a spouse or parent. Hope in the Divine future that embraces our lives awakens us to new possibilities and challenges us to choose life and love even in difficult situations.

7.   *Serenity*

Many people vacillate between feelings of impotence and omnipotence. On the one hand, we feel helpless to change ourselves or the world. On the other hand, we feel an exaggerated responsibility for everything.

Recently, Bruce was approached by a woman at a wedding reception who told him about her experience of becoming a student of a new age guru. The guru's constant mantra was, "You create your own reality." For a while, this mental omnipotence worked for her. But when she experienced some personal setbacks, including alienation from her best friend, her teacher told her, "You chose this break up. You are responsible for the situation that created your friend's anger. Your life in its entirety mirrors your negative thoughts."

The spirit of serenity arises from knowing that we *don't* have to do everything ourselves. As the American philosopher William James stated, the practical meaning of God's existence is that we can take a "moral holiday" from time to time. We can relax with the trust that life will go on and that others will take our place in the quest for justice and wholeness. We are not in control of some of the most important things in life. We can't fully ensure our children's safety, our physical and emotional health, or the kinds of people our children will become when they're on their own. Still, our day-to-day actions can promote health and wholeness. In the spirit of the "butterfly effect," even the smallest acts of freedom can transform our lives and bring beauty to the world.

Perhaps, no one has described the dynamics of serenity better than twentieth-century Christian theologian Reinhold Niebuhr:

> God, give us the grace to accept with serenity the things that cannot be changed, courage to change the things which should be changed, and the wisdom to distinguish the one from the other.

Nearly two hundred years earlier, Rabbi Yechiel of Zlotkov related this same spiritual wisdom:

There are two things you shouldn't worry about. That which is impossible to fix and that which is possible to fix. What is impossible to fix, how will worrying help? That which is possible to fix, why worry, just fix it![12]

Serenity emerges when we recognize that we are never alone and that God is with us to guide and protect us and those we love. In such moments, we claim our authentic, though limited, power to be co-creators with God.

Serenity is the gift of the quiet mind. In the upheavals of life, as the psalmist reminds us, we can "be still," for in the stillness we will discover Divine guidance and the wisdom to find our way home.

8.   Sabbath

Today, physicians and spiritual guides tell us that most people suffer from "hurry sickness" or "time deficiency syndrome." Our lives are ruled by the ticking clock. We never have enough time to balance work, family, self-care, and recreation. Even our vacations take on a frenetic pace. Armed with video and digital cameras, we record each sight for posterity as we go from one attraction to the next. In between sightseeing and balancing our needs with our children and grandchildren's demands, we check our e-mail and voice mail, and make notes on our digital organizers, worried that we will fall behind our co-workers or miss something of great consequence. As we look at the

12 Simcha Raz, *Hasidic Wisdom: Sayings from the Jewish Sages,* translated by Dov Peretz Elkins and Jonathan Elkins (Northdale, NJ: Jason Aronson, 1997), p. 101.

clock, we are ruled by the vision of scarcity. Our lives are governed by "deadlines" rather than "lifelines." We forget the abundant life that is all around us as we hurry from one moment to another. Even our children's days are filled with ceaseless activity as we drive them from soccer practice to computer class and then on to martial arts. But there is hope for the soccer mom and dad and the harried grandparent. Time won't stand still, but we can experience time from a new perspective: fullness, abundance, peace, and the wonder of God's eternal presence.

New Testament Greek describes time by the words *chronos* and *kairos*. *Chronos* time is the evenly flowing clock time. Measured, calculated, and digitalized, it is always flowing away from us. It measures our life from birth to death. It is punctuated by deadlines and terminus points. *Chronos* time constantly lives in the shadow of eventual death. But there is another dimension of time, *kairos* time, which is the fullness of time, the time of God's presence that undergirds chronological time. *Kairos* time is holy time that reminds us that our lives take place in an eternal context where change is balanced by constancy, and death is the prelude to everlasting life.

In the biblical tradition, the primary antidote to hurry sickness is the Sabbath. The Sabbath is a sanctuary of time that enables us to experience holiness even in the most frenetic schedules. Though most of our schedules don't permit a literal twenty-four hour Sabbath, still there is a great deal of wisdom in the biblical image of Sabbath, whether we practice it on Friday, Saturday, or Sunday, or with several mini-sabbaths during the week. In words that liberate us from the constraints of watches and schedules, the biblical tradition affirms the importance of resting mind, body, and spirit for health and wholeness:

Remember the sabbath day and keep it holy.
Six days you shall labor and do all your work.
But the seventh day is a sabbath to the Lord
your God; you shall not do any work—you,
your son or your daughter. . . . For in six days
the Lord made heaven and earth, the sea, and
all that is in them, but rested the seventh
day; therefore the Lord blessed the sabbath
day and consecrated it. (Exodus 20:8-11)

According to the Bible, even God rested! The Divine
Parent, like the good human parent, creates an open space
for creation's children to grow and play and explore their
own creative possibilities. Sabbath time reminds us of the
wisdom of doing nothing, of the importance of balancing
the outer journey of holy and loving action with the inner
journey of open receptivity and listening. When we, as
God's partners in creation, make room for Sabbath time,
our lives become infused with new energy and vitality. We
gain a larger perspective on our lives and discover what is
truly important and what is expendable.

As Abraham Joshua Heschel proclaims, Sabbath is a
sanctuary of time that enables us to experience the holiness
of time moment by moment. Sabbath time is the path to
peace. Though time is perpetually perishing, we can discover
its amazing abundance as we practice hourly, daily, weekly,
monthly, and yearly Sabbaths. In Sabbath time, we can experience the moments of even our busiest days as reflections of
Divine eternity. In everyday life, we can experience the Sabbath simply by holy breathing. One of Bruce's spiritual men-
tors, Alan Armstrong Hunter, advised his students to
"breathe the spirit deeply in" and then breathe whatever
stress or anxiety "out again." In like manner, Vietnamese
Buddhist monk Thich Naht Hanh affirms this in his own

breath prayer, "Breathing in I feel peace; breathing out I smile," which can be simply abbreviated "peace" and "smile." These Sabbath moments remind us that we are always on Holy Ground. As children of eternity, we always have enough time to do what is truly important in life.

Daily Sabbath moments of prayer and meditation can transform our experience of time. While stress arises from and contributes to the prison house of time, meditation and prayer connect us with God's time that is ever creative, ever renewing, and everlasting. Once a week, it is good to take a longer Sabbath. After completing his pastoral duties on Sunday morning, Bruce devotes the rest of the day to relaxation and recreation with friends and family. Lew spends his Saturdays in rest and reflection. A walk in the woods, a good book, a longer session of meditation, supper with friends transform our time and refresh us for the challenges ahead.

Sabbath invites us to claim the year-round adventure of holy days as well during Rosh Hashanah, Yom Kippur, Passover, Christmas, and Easter. Sabbath invites us to see all the seasons of the year, whether religious seasons, such as Advent, or national holidays, such as Thanksgiving and Martin Luther King, Jr.'s birthday, as openings to the holiness of God's time. A monthly retreat day or weekend for prayer and reflection can give perspective to both the past and future. A yearly retreat can awaken us to the eternity from which all things arise and to which all things return. If we live by Sabbath time, even *chronos* time becomes a friend as we discover that there is always enough time for love, beauty, excellence, and creativity.

Ultimately, Sabbath reminds us that wholeness arises from a flexible balance between work and play, company and solitude, speaking and listening, rest and action.

Every part of our being needs the spiritual nourishment that comes from living in light of an eternal Sabbath.

9.   *Love*

Love is our primary spiritual resource. In his famous hymn to love, the apostle Paul proclaims, "Faith, hope, and love abide, these three; and the greatest of these is love" (1 Corinthians 13:13). In the spirit of his Jewish parents, Jesus affirmed the words of Leviticus 19:18, "Love your neighbor as yourself." The New Testament asserts that "perfect love casts out fear" (1 John 4:18) and that only those who truly live by love can experience God's presence in the world (1 John 4:7).

Love tells us that we cannot be whole until everyone else is healed. In the spirit of Jesus' parable, the shepherd journeys into the darkest night in search of the one lost sheep. When the sheep is found, he rejoices because apart from that one lost sheep the hundred in the sheepfold are incomplete (Luke 15:1-7). The circle of love embraces everyone without exception.

Love invites us to feel the pain and joy of the other. Rabbi Moshe Leib of Sassov, the Sassover Rebbe who lived two centuries ago, captured the essence of love in action in his recollection of a conversation he overheard between two peasants:

> The first peasant asked his neighbor, "Tell me, do you love me?"
>
> His friend responded, "Certainly, I love you. I love you like a brother."
>
> Shaking his head, the first peasant countered, "You don't love me. You don't know what I lack. You don't know what I need."

As Moshe Leib so well understood, "To see the need of others and to bear the burden of their sorrow, that is true love."[13]

Love is the art of connection that inspires us to seek the welfare of others as if it is our own well-being. When Jesus said, "Just as you did it to one of the least of these . . . you did it to me," he was expressing the deep spiritual truth that everything we do is our gift to God (Matthew 25:40). But, more than that, Jesus affirmed that the Holy One comes to us in every encounter and every person we meet. All boulders, even the most jagged and painful, are bursting forth with angels. All persons show us a glimpse of what Mother Teresa described as "God in all of the Divine's distressing disguises."

In his parable of the last judgment, Jesus described God's response to those who seek to love their neighbors as themselves:

> "Come, you that are blessed by my Father,
> inherit the kingdom prepared for you from
> the foundation of the world; for I was hungry
> and you gave me food, I was thirsty and you
> gave me something to drink, I was a stranger
> and you welcomed me, I was naked and you
> gave me clothing, I was sick and you visited
> me." Then the righteous will answer him,
> "Lord, when was it that we saw you hungry
> and gave you food, or thirsty and gave you
> something to drink? And when was it that
> we saw you a stranger and welcomed you, or
> naked and gave you clothing? And when was

13 Adapted from Maurice Friedman, *A Dialogue with Hasidic Tales: Hallowing the Everyday* (New York: Insight Books, 1988), p. 86.

it that we saw you sick or in prison and vis-
ited you?" And the king will answer them,
"Truly I tell you, just as you did it to one of
the least of these who are members of my
family, you did it to me." (Matthew
25:34-40)

Centuries before Jesus' inspiring words, the author
of Proverbs captured the universality of God's love embodied in our daily acts of kindness: "If your enemies are hungry, give them bread to eat; if they are thirsty, give them
water to drink" (Proverbs 25:21). No person exists beyond
the circle of God's love and our care. God comes to us anon-
ymously every day. Without being aware of it, we may be
the answer to someone's prayer. We may be the angel sent
from heaven to help them find their way.

At the heart of love is the choice to live by compassion and connection. Simply put, love enables us to experience the world from our neighbor's perspective. Our
compassion reflects God's own compassion, the Divine receptivity of the One to whom all hearts are open and all desires known.

10. Forgiveness

Forgiveness is love in action. The power of forgiveness is revealed in the biblical story of Joseph and his brothers (Genesis 37-45). In their jealousy over Joseph's
relationship with their father, Jacob, Joseph's brothers
threw him into a well and then sold him to slave traders,
who eventually sold him into bondage in Egypt. Because Joseph had the gift of interpreting dreams, Joseph became a
free man and a leader in the Egyptian government. Years
later he was reunited with his brothers, when they came to
Egypt seeking food to ease the burden of the severe famine.

While they did not recognize their brother, he recognized them. He forgave them of the past and invited them to settle with him in Egypt.

Forgiveness sets us free to love and create a new reality with old enemies. Letting go of the past, we are able to embrace a creative future in which our wounds become the basis for a new beginning. Trusting in the goodness of the universe transforms us from frightened competitors to large-souled lovers who can transform antagonists into future partners.

In the final days of the Civil War, when it had become clear that the Confederacy would be vanquished, Abraham Lincoln was asked, "What are you going to do with the South now that they've been defeated?" His questioner expected Lincoln to outline a policy of punishment and humiliation. Much to his surprise, the President responded, "I'll treat them as if they never have left."

The prophet Isaiah spoke of the forgiveness embodied by God's Suffering Servant: "I gave my back to those who struck me, and my cheeks to those who pulled out the beard; I did not hide my face from insulting and spitting. The Lord God helps me; therefore I have not been disgraced; therefore I have set my face like flint, and I know that I shall not be put to shame" (Isaiah 50:6-7). Jesus' Sermon on the Mount counseled, "Blessed are the peacemakers, for they will be called children of God" (Matthew 5:9).

Forgiveness is central to both Judaism and Christianity, although each tradition views the role of the wrong-doer differently. Many Christians do not see the wrong-doer's repentance as a prerequisite for the victim granting forgiveness. The ability to ask for forgiveness is often a response to the surprising Divine and human love we have received. In the Jewish tradition, the wrong-doer must do something positive, undertake a transformation, *teshuvah*, to overcome the transgression.

Still, forgiveness is not a virtue for the faint-hearted, nor does forgiveness imply that we allow others to abuse, manipulate, or oppress. The open-hearted spirit of forgiveness arises from a deep sense of self-affirmation and personal integrity. We can forgive precisely because we know that God is with us in the conflict.

Forgiveness is grounded in God's love for all creatures. Again, in the Sermon on the Mount, Jesus enjoined his disciples to see forgiveness as a way of life, shaping our response to every encounter:

> You have heard that it was said, "You shall love your neighbor and hate your enemy." But I say to you, Love your enemies and pray for those who persecute you, so that you may be children of your Father in heaven; for [God] makes his sun rise on the evil and on the good, and sends rain on the righteous and on the unrighteous. (Matthew 5:43-45)

Jesus was once asked how often a person should a person forgive her or his neighbor. His inquisitor thought seven times was enough. Jesus responded with "not seven times, but, I tell you, seventy-seven times" (Matthew 18:22). We are to forgive each other infinitely, just as God infinitely forgives us. For Jesus, these were not mere words. As he was dying on the cross, abandoned even by his friends, Jesus embraced his persecutors and offered them a path to healing: "Father, forgive them; for they do not know what they are doing" (Luke 23:34).

Forgiveness is not confined to absolving the perpetrator; it is about healing the victim. Forgiveness creates a field of healing force that can change a relationship, a city, or a nation. We marvel at the healing power of forgiveness in South Africa. When Nelson Mandela was freed from prison, many expected him to punish his Afrikaaner oppressors. Instead, Mandela set out to heal the alienation that had defined South Africa during the twentieth century. Reconciliation involved the acknowledgment of injustice, but it also meant the willingness to forgive and begin again. In the spirit of Martin Luther King, Jr., Mandela knew that national healing required personal and social healing. In the healing hologram, part and whole are inextricably connected. Healing occurs one moment at a time. But small acts of healing eventually transform the whole as well as the parts.

Corrie ten Boom, author of *The Hiding Place*, lost her entire family in the Holocaust concentration camps. Though she wasn't Jewish, her family was arrested for providing safe haven for Jewish families fleeing Germany. After the war, Corrie ten Boom became famous for her reflections on her struggle to remain a faithful servant of God even in the concentration camp. Following one of her speeches, she recognized a man who had been a Gestapo officer in the camp where her sister died. He came up to her with tears in his eyes, sharing his need for forgiveness. He did not recognize her at first. As she gazed upon him, Corrie felt paralyzed with anger and hatred. She couldn't even raise her hand to shake his trembling hand. She did not want to forgive him. But, then she heard the inner voice of Christ, reminding her of how much God had forgiven her. With tears in her eyes, Corrie ten Boom embraced her former captor. Ancient enemies had become companions in the journey toward healing.

Sometimes, when the pain and betrayal is so great that we cannot face it alone, forgiveness requires a healing community. We may need to seek the companionship of a spiritual leader, therapist, intimate friend, or support group to find the courage and strength to forgive and love again. Forgiveness does not require us to be perfect, but just to be open to our deep connectedness with God and healing friends. In that deep interdependence, we may discover the angel not only within ourselves but also within those persons whom we must forgive in order to move on with our lives.

Our commitment to forgiveness enables us to become God's partners in the restoration of all things, in *tikkun olam*, in mending the world. Through forgiveness, we can begin to heal the brokenness of creation one moment at a time.

CHAPTER FOUR

Tools for Spiritual Transformation

OD calls us to be the artists of our experience. Like Michelangelo, we can sculpt from the rough-hewn materials of our lives a unique work of beauty and grace. But, like every artist, we cannot fully control the materials with which we work. The materials from which we create a life of meaning and service may come as the fruits of a lifetime of decision-making, or as pleasant surprises, but they may also come unbidden and unwanted. The boulders from which we sculpt our lives may truly be jagged, painful, and misshapen. From time to time, the burden of fashioning something beautiful of our lives may seem almost too heavy to bear. But even from these most challenging boulders, we can create a life of grace, dignity, and wonder because God is with us, constantly luring us forward by the dream of who we may become as co-creators in God's Holy Adventure.

Every successful artist must know the materials with which he or she works. To bring forth an angel from the jagged boulder, Michelangelo used certain tools as his instruments of creative transformation. These tools enabled him to shape the boulders into works of enduring beauty. Our faith traditions have given us spiritual tools that enable us to bring forth beauty from the challenges of our lives: prayer, meditation, healing imagination, and spiritual affirmation.

These tools enable us to recover our deepest spiritual center. In the stillness of quiet communion with the Holy One, we can see the pattern and hear the voice of a deeper reality within the chaos of our momentary experience. While our traditions have given ample guidance to spiritual artists and adventurers in the past, we need to reclaim these tools for our time. In the pages that follow, we offer some tools for spiritual transformation that are emerging from the new partnership of progressive Jews and Christians. While universal in scope, these tools find their embodiment in each person's unique experience. It is important to find the spiritual practices that work for you—that fit your personality, lifestyle, ethnicity, gender, age, and spiritual longings—as you experiment with, personalize, or go beyond these particular disciplines of spiritual transformation.

The Circle of Prayer

Prayer is the ultimate tool for personal and social transformation. While illness and tragedy tend to constrict our experience and isolate us from other people and our deeper selves, prayer places us at the Divine Center. The very act of praying connects us with a larger vision of ourselves and the world. The intention to pray reminds us that we are always in God's hands. No one knows how prayer "works," but again and again it has been found that those who pray experience greater energy, peace, and comfort in difficult times. They find new insights with which to respond to the tragedies and complexities of life.

Prayer is an act of ecological affirmation. Prayer reminds us that we are intricately connected with God and with all of reality. The Divine Center unites us with every other center in the dynamic web of relationships that constitutes the universe. Non-local in nature, our prayers radiate across the universe, creating a healing and affirmative field of force that transforms ourselves and those for whom we pray. Each prayerful thought and meditative moment positively changes the spiritual environment that surrounds us and those for whom we pray. Our prayers are the "soul food" that nourishes our spirits and our partners in prayer.

People constantly ask us, "How shall we pray?" Jesus' own disciples begged him, "Teach us to pray," and the Healer responded with the words, "Our [Mother/Father] in heaven, hallowed be your name" (Matthew 6:9). For Jews and Christians alike, God is profoundly personal, mothering and fathering all things with a creative and responsive love. Like the best of parents, God's love has no requirements. No specific prayer form is necessary in order to communicate with the Divine Parent. A drowning woman does not need to recite theological doctrines to reach the attention of the Divine Companion. Simply a panic-stricken "help" is enough to alert the One whose desire is to serve and save all creation.

In the matrix of events that constitute our lives, God responds to us just as we are. As one spiritual guide noted, "Pray as you can, not as you can't." The still, small voice of God whispers to us in the chaos of our lives, inviting us to pause awhile and center ourselves in the Loving Center that centers us. Whether we recite the traditional liturgical prayers of Judaism or Christianity, burst forth with extemporaneous thanksgiving and praise, or use visualizations to support our healing and the growth of others, prayer changes things. God is ready to respond to our deepest needs even before we ask. In fact, our very asking is inspired by the Divine Love that grounds each thought and feeling. Still, our asking opens our hearts to the abundant assistance that is always here for us.

❀ *A ROAD MAP FOR PRAYER*

Many of us like directions. We feel more comfortable when we have a road map for the adventure ahead. While the road to prayer has many unexpected turns and alternative routes, our traditions have pointed us toward a number of ways of praying, including verbal, silent, imaginative, or melodic forms. While not exhaustive, the road map of prayer includes five core aspects: adoration, confession, thanksgiving, supplication, and surrender.

1.   Adoration

Adoration is the affirmation of the wonder of the universe and the loving wisdom of its Creator. With each new day, we can proclaim, "This is the day that [God] has made; let us rejoice and be glad in it" (Psalm 118:24). Adoration reflects what Abraham Joshua Heschel has described as our "radical amazement" at life itself in all its intricacy and beauty. According the biblical tradition, all things praise God at their depths, and the universe is a symphony of joyful adoration.

What would our daily life be like if we began each day in the spirit of Psalm 148?

Praise the Eternal One!

Praise the Holy One from the heavens, praise God in the heights.

Praise God, all the divine angels, praise the Holy One, all creation.

Praise God, sun and moon; praise the Supreme Sovereign, all you shining stars!

Praise the Eternal, you highest heavens, and you waters above the heavens!

Praise the Holy One from the earth, you sea monsters and all deeps,

Fire and hail, snow and frost, stormy wind fulfilling God's command!

Mountains and hills, fruit trees and all cedars!

Wild animals and all cattle, creeping things and flying birds.

Leaders of the earth and all peoples, all rulers of the earth!

Young men and women alike, old and young together.

What would our lives be like if we joined with Psalm 150's hymn of creation in bursting forth with each sunrise, "Let everything that breathes praise God!"

In the spirit of Louis Armstrong's oft-recorded song, adoration gives us eyes to see a "wonderful world" in our children, parents, spouses—even in the complexity and challenges of each new day. With the Native American spiritual tradition, adoration of God's wonderful creation within us and beyond us proclaims, "With beauty all around us, we walk." Adoration and praise affirm the wonder of our bodies, minds, spirits, and relationships and open us to the Divine adventure of a surprising cosmos.

2. Confession

While many people identify confession with the pathological guilt that has alienated many from religion, authentic confession is simply sharing our lives with God with full awareness of our wonder as well as our imperfection. Confession is a call to healing and transformation, not punishment. No one can make confession without the hope that the One who hears is willing to accept us just as we are, even as that Holy One calls us forward to new possibilities.

Confession is the gift of self-awareness that frees us from the prison of the past and the temptation to hide our deepest reality from ourselves and others. Psalm 139:23-24 captures the essence of confession with this prayer:

> Search me, O God, and know my heart; test me and know my thoughts. See if there is any wicked way in me, and lead me in the way everlasting.

By being honest with God, we can be honest with ourselves and with those we love. We confess because we are loved and because we know that our hope of healing arises from the weaving together our self-awareness with our awareness of God's eternal affirmation and care. In confession, we let go of the burdens of the past, commit ourselves to reconciliation with others in the present, and embrace the freedom of the future.

3. *Thanksgiving*

The German mystic Meister Eckhardt proclaimed that "if the only prayer you make is a prayer of thanksgiving, that will be sufficient." Thanksgiving roots us in the abundance of the universe. When we are thankful, we are never alone. We experience our lives as arising out of an intricate web of holy relationships. While we still recognize the imperfections of life and ourselves, we can see these imperfections as the evolving shadow side of a world grounded in love and beauty. Thanksgiving enables us to see abundance where others see scarcity.

Gratitude is both an individual and a relational spiritual resource. Think about your day today: How often did you express your appreciation to your spouse, child, parent, a co-worker, a waiter or waitress, or a dear friend? How often did you simply thank God for the gift of life and the blessings of this day? Thanksgiving reminds us that without the care of others, we would neither exist nor flourish. Thanksgiving is an antidote to hopelessness and self-centeredness. In sharing our appreciation for ordinary kindness, our gratitude nurtures others' self-affirmation and our connectedness to the goodness of life.

Try this experiment in thankfulness:

- Take a few moments just to be still and remember the beauty of life.
- Let yourself spontaneously complete this simple sentence: *"I am thankful for _____."*
- Keep going for a few minutes, adding to your list those persons, experiences, and events that come to mind. The possibilities for gratitude are virtually endless: the love of parents, your partner's smile and affirmation, your child's artwork and trust, your

health and intelligence, the creativity that inspires
you, the gift of birth in a country that nurtures
freedom and initiative, a friend's prayers and
support, a transformed relationship, the sunset and
cherry blossoms, the protective care of firefighters
and police officers.

♦ Visualize each person or event for which you are
thankful. As you see their faces, silently say "thank
you" to them for the joy and meaning they have
brought to your life.

♦ As you conclude, gratefully lift up your heart to the
Eternal One for the wonder of your life and all
creation, and for bringing your loved ones into your
life. In the silence, make a commitment not only to
be thankful but to speak and act your thanksgiving.

4.   *Supplication*

The old-fashioned word "supplication" embraces
prayers for ourselves and for others. Prayers of supplication
are profoundly concrete. We may pray for the safety of a soldier in a far off country or a child at school, even as we pray
for peace and justice in the world. We may pray for the healing of a friend's marriage as we pray for an end to the violence in Israel and Palestine.

We cannot, however, predict the outcome of our
prayers. Our prayers do not force God's hand or persuade an
apparently uncaring God to help the ones we love. The Eternal is not an outside spectator who supernaturally intervenes to change the course of events unilaterally. Prayer is
not magic or manipulation, but rather an openness to our
role in incarnating God's vision for ourselves and our
planet. Because God is the immanent artist of love, con-

stantly moving within our lives and the world, weaving together our freedom and creativity for the well-being of all things, God's answer to prayer includes not just our wishes but God's vision of wholeness for our friends, family, community, nation, and the planet. Prayer reflects our willingness to become creative partners with God in bringing healing and beauty to the world.

As an affirmation of our profound connection with life, prayer transforms our self-understanding and opens us to new possibilities. Even if our prayers do not initially seem to change anything, they *do* transform our perception of reality. Mindful prayer awakens us to the relationship between our well-being and the well-being of others. We discover that our desires and needs are profoundly different in light of the needs of the hungry and dispossessed. We come to recognize the relationship between our own well-being and the healthy ecology of the planet and its citizens.

Jesus once said, "I am vine, you are the branches. Those who abide in me and I in them, bear much fruit" (John 15:5). God's healing energy flows through all things, urging everything toward wholeness and adventure. Prayers of supplication, both for ourselves and for others, weave together silence, words, and images as a means of opening to this Divine vitality and hopefulness. In connecting with Divine energy through prayer, we awaken to the enduring spiritual resources of *hope, serenity,* and *forgiveness,* and nurture them in the lives of others.

To pray for greater *hopefulness* in a time of challenge, close your eyes and rest in God's presence. In the silence, repeat a prayerful affirmation, such as one of those offered below, allowing the words to connect you to your deepest reality. If your mind wanders, simply bring it back to your prayer without judgment. You may even choose to pray for the thoughts that randomly emerge. Even random thoughts contain seeds of insight and inspiration. We have found the following brief prayers of hopeful supplication helpful in our own spiritual journeys:

- *"God, supply me with an abundance of joy."*
- *"God, fill my mind, heart, and soul with joyfulness."*
- *"Eternal One, help me let go of limits and open to Divine possibilities."*
- *"God, remove all the shadows from my being and fill me with hope and optimism."*
- *"Loving One, help me let go of the past and open to your bright and hopeful future."*

In times of stress, anxiety, or impatience, prayers for *serenity* can help us recover a peaceful spiritual center. After taking deep breaths, with your eyes closed, repeat one of the following petitions for peace and serenity:

- *"Holy God, help me to let go of my stress [anger, impatience, envy, etc.] and grant me a tranquil nature."*
- *"Purify my heart and mind, O Loving One, so that I may serve you in truth, humility, and joyfulness."*
- *"God, fill me with your spirit of peace and tranquility."*
- *"God, make me an instrument of your peace."*

Forgiveness arises from our willingness to open ourselves to God's reconciling love. In choosing to see angels in boulders, we dissolve our fear, hatred, and anger. This new perception of reality heals our emotions as well as our relationships. The following prayers join Divine and human for-giveness in reconciliation:

- *"Loving God, help me to see _____ through your eyes of love. Help me to let go of judgment and guilt in my relationship with her (or him)."*
- *"God, help me to let go of the painful past, and open my heart to your loving future."*
- *"God, let your love flow through me to bring healing and love to everyone I meet."*

5.   Surrender

Sometimes the best form of prayer is simply one of surrender, the acceptance that "God's will be done" in a particular situation. Perhaps you have thought about how you should pray for a friend, whose cancer had spread throughout her body. "Should I pray for a cure or a gentle death?" you ask. In such situations, the answer is never clear. We never fully know what is best for ourselves or any other person. But there are two prayers we can always pray: the simple statement, "Thy will be done," which joins our prayers consciously and unconsciously with the intentions of God for this particular person; and the simple request, "God, heal my friend," which embraces not only the possibility of a temporary physical cure, but also a sense of peace and wholeness that extends beyond this lifetime.

Many people have found peace of mind through prayers of surrender. To surrender to God's care for our lives is a positive action, not an evasion of responsibility. It is letting go of our particular agenda and letting the Holy Adventure lead the way.

Prayers of surrender remind us of our limitations

and our need for a larger perspective on life. Though they seem unfocused in nature, non-directed and open-ended prayers of surrender have the power to change our lives. Simply to say, "Thy will be done" or "God, let it be," opens our hearts to the highest good for ourselves and others in harmony with God's purposes. Non-directed prayers of surrender are empowering acts of trust in the One who truly knows what is best for all things.

Here are some prayers of surrender you can bring to the God who is infinitely resourceful:

- *"Into your hand, O Loving God, I commit my life. Your love has made me whole. I have slept, and now I wake, for you sustain me. "*

- *"Holy God, I open to your loving guidance. Show me what I should do today. Teach me what I should say today. I will follow your guidance wherever it leads me."*

- *"Holy God, I commit my loved one to your care. I place her (or him) in your hands. I know that nothing can separate her (or him) from your love. Help me be an instrument of love in her (or his) life."*

- *"_____ dwells in the circle of Divine love. He/she is safe in God's care."*

- *"I trust the future of _____ to God's protection and care. The One who loved them into life will also receive them in death."*

While prayers of surrender may simply involve silent listening for God's still, small voice, these open, yet seeking, prayers may be nurtured by supplications, such as:

- *"Show me the way, dear God."*
- *"I need your guidance and wisdom, Eternal One."*
- *"I awaken to your perfect will in this situation."*
- *"Give _____ the healing that is right and good for this time in their lives."*

Often we need to open ourselves to a deeper insight or wisdom than our own. However, the quiet receptivity of prayer may lead to action. Every good artist recognizes the need to join activity and receptivity in her or his work. In opening to God's wisdom, we may receive clear directives for life-changing actions.

As the saying goes, "Pray as if everything depends on God, and act as if everything depends on you." On the other hand, prayer is the ultimate act of connection. It can also be the ultimate inspiration to act on behalf of others. In our prayers, we may discover that we are the answer to someone else's prayers. In our openness to God's gentle grace and infinite wisdom, we discover that prayer is not only a state of mind, but permeates our actions, emotions, and even our bodies.

❀ PRAYING WITH OUR BODIES

There is one additional avenue of prayer that many people don't consider—praying with our bodies. The heavens declare the glory of God and so do our bodies. While some religious traditions identify holiness with celibacy and mistrust of the body, Judaism and Christianity proclaim that the body in its wholeness is good and worthy of love. Every body is an incarnation of Divine creativity. Mind and body, spirit and flesh are woven together in the fabric of the Holy Adventure. All prayer is body prayer.

We can discover God's presence as we kneel in prayer or raise our hands in joy. For some of us, counting prayer beads, praying the rosary, bowing down in prayer, or making the sign of the cross awakens us to the invisible God whose presence permeates all things. Through creative body prayer, we affirm that our bodies, in whatever form and health condition we find ourselves, are created by Divine love and are sacraments of beauty and wisdom.

A simple touch—a hug, holding someone, putting an arm around the shoulder—can become a prayer for healing. We can experience God's healing presence in rituals such as anointing with oil and the laying on of hands in times of worship, or through more formal types of healing work, such as therapeutic touch or Reiki touch healing. When we dedicate our touch to God, every touch is a prayer.

Ordinary daily rituals, such as meals, can also become prayers. While some of us feel uncomfortable with ritualistic table graces, we have come to appreciate the value of quiet thanksgiving and mindfulness as we eat our meals. In Judaism and Christianity, we celebrate Divine and human companionship as we share meals with friends and family at the Passover Seder, the Sabbath Meal, the Easter and Christmas celebrations, church potluck dinners, or Holy Communion. These special meals remind us that God is present as our guest and host at every meal time.

One way to awaken to God's presence at our meals is to pray in advance for our dinner companions. When one of Bruce's friends, Sarah, prepares a meal for her family or friends, she visualizes each one as she chops vegetables or makes dessert. She sees each one of her future dining partners as being surrounded and permeated by Divine light and visualizes the meal ahead as joyful and loving.

Some of us "sweat our prayers." If you are a person who walks in the morning or evening, try this form of bodily prayer. With each step, envisage God's healing light radiating through your body from your head to the soles of your feet. As you experience the Divine light, proclaim an affirmation for each part of your body, such as:

- *"God's light fills my mind and gives me clarity."*
- *"My immune system is strong and effective."*
- *"My heart is strong and healthy. My blood pressure is sound and regular."*
- *"God's light brings health to my reproductive system and my sexual activity."*
- *"God is healing my [name a particular part of your body] so I can serve and bless others in health and wholeness."*

We proclaim our original wholeness by bringing Divine grace to every bodily activity, from sexuality and birth, to family meals and a child's first steps, to the hug of a friend and a lover's kiss. With Eric Liddel, the hero of the film *Chariots of Fire* who joyfully claimed, "God made me fast, and when I run, I feel God's pleasure," we can celebrate God's gifts and share God's pleasure in our bodies. Our bodies are not misshapen boulders, but temples of the Divine Spirit, reflecting the same love that was embodied in the Healer Jesus and in the first movements of creation. A spirituality of Shalom reminds us that we "live, move, and have our being" in the circle of Divine love. Every part of us—body, mind, and spirit—arises from Divine inspiration and returns to Divine remembrance.

The Path of Meditation

African-American mystic Howard Thurman tells the story of the power of silence. One day, young Howard went berry picking in the woods behind his grandmother's house. In search of luscious red berries, he plunged deeper and deeper into the woods. His berry-picking adventure was cut short when he heard the boom of thunder and noticed that the sky was darkening. Nothing around him looked familiar. He became panic-stricken and almost bolted further into the unknown woods. Then he remembered the counsel of his grandmother: "When you don't know where you are, be still and size up the situation." In the quiet, young Howard took a deep breath and began to look all around. With each flash of lightning, he looked to the right and left, the front and the back, until he finally saw something familiar. Step by step, he followed the lightning flashes until he found his way home.

Meditation is taking the time to be still, to find the path of silent awareness. Wide awake, yet physically relaxed, meditation calms both the body and mind. The stillness of meditation clears the mind of its ongoing, often chaotic chatter and enables us to enter into a spacious silence where we can hear the voice of God speaking through our thoughts and feelings. There we can regain our connection to the Source of All and invite a greater peace and creativity into our daily life.

The author of Psalm 46 reminds us that even in the most stressful times we can discover God's presence through quiet prayer and meditation. Even when the earth is shaking and our spirits under siege, we can discover a deep spiritual stillness. When we are connected to God through prayer and meditation, God's wisdom and power permeate our thoughts and actions. As the Psalmist counsels, "Be still, and know that I am God" (Psalm 46:10).

The Quakers have given us the simplest form of meditation. Inspired by the vision of God as the inner light of all persons, they simply listen for God's spirit speaking within the individual at the Quaker meeting. In profound stillness, they wait to hear the voice of God speaking beneath all the surface voices. In the spirit of the Quakers, your form of meditation may be choosing simply to be still, knowing that beneath your passing thoughts there is the deeper reality of Divine Silence. But, in that same spirit, if you hear the voice of God whispering in the silence, you are called eventually to share your insight with others in word or action.

Many of us need a more focused form of meditation because the spacious silence gets drowned out by our constant inner dialogue. A simple breath prayer may quiet your mind and open your spirit:

✿ *A SIMPLE BREATH PRAYER*

- ♦ With each inhaling, rest in the words, "I breathe the spirit deeply in."
- ♦ As you exhale, let go of stress and anxiety.
- ♦ Place your burdens and stresses in the vastness of Divine Care.

Meditation provides us with a mini-sabbath in the midst of a busy day. The quiet mind that is achieved through meditation contributes to a healthy body, and the health of the body reverberates in mental well-being. Many Westerners first encountered meditation in the sixties and early seventies through Maharishi Mahesh Yogi's Transcendental Meditation, and later through Herbert Benson's Relaxation Response. Benson found that practicing virtually any form of meditation, whether sacred or secular, for fifteen to twenty minutes twice a day lowers blood pressure, relieves stress, and enhances immune functioning. We are, as Benson suggests, "wired for God."[14] Simply put, the most basic form of the Relaxation Response involves the following steps:

❀ *RELAXATION RESPONSE*

• Sit in a comfortable position with your eyes closed.
• Let your body relax, starting with your face and moving to your feet.
• Focus on a word or phrase as you inhale and exhale.
• Gently respond to distractions by simply bringing your attention back to your focus word without judgment.
• Continue with your focus word for 15-20 minutes.
• Conclude by gently bringing your attention back to the room, opening your eyes and getting up when you feel rested.
• Practice twice daily, usually morning and late afternoon or evening.

Many people have found great value in using words of faith as their meditative focus, rather than the unfamiliar Sanskrit words employed in Transcendental Meditation or the secular words of the Relaxation Response. Catholic spiritual guides Basil Pennington and Thomas Keating have described these meaningful prayers as "Centering Prayer." Similar to the Relaxation Response, this ancient meditative

14 Herbert Benson, *Timeless Healing: Power and Biology of Belief* (New York: Scribner, 1996), p. 206.

form, adapted to modern needs, is composed of the following steps:

❀ *CENTERING PRAYER*

+ Find a comfortable position and close your eyes.
+ Say a brief prayer of openness or thanksgiving.
+ Focus on a simple word, such as "love," "God," "*Shalom,*" "*Shema Israel,*" "*tikkun olam,*" "peace," "light," "*hokmah,*" "Christ," "health."
+ When your mind wanders, simply bring your mind back to the meditative focus without judgment.
+ After 15-20 minutes, simply conclude with a brief prayer of gratitude.

Some people worry about falling asleep while they are meditating. If you have any time concerns related to meditation, try setting the alarm on your clock ahead twenty-five minutes to some gentle music of reawakening. While many people are so fatigued that sleep may be the most healthful response at a given time, using an alarm clock minimizes a focus on time that might interfere with your quality of meditation.

In the spirit of Centering Prayer, the great Hasidic teacher Rabbi Nachman of Breslov encouraged people simply to repeat the phrase "Master of the Universe" or "*Ribbono shel Olam*" as a meditative device. Rabbi Nachman believed that the repetition of this simple phrase enabled people to achieve the higher awareness that comes from encountering God. You may also choose to repeat traditional prayers such as the *Shema* or the Lord's Prayer to focus and awaken your mind to your inner spiritual treasure.

The spiritual classic of the Russian Orthodox Church, *The Way of the Pilgrim*, invites spiritual seekers to pray without ceasing the words of the Jesus Prayer, "Lord, Jesus Christ, Son of God, have mercy upon me a sinner." This prayer may be abbreviated to "Lord, have mercy," or simply, "mercy." In any case, this prayer, which can be modified to embrace the spirit of Judaism, awakens us to the experience of our constant interdependence with God and our continual need for Divine care and refreshment.

Meditation, like prayer, cannot be limited to one form or technique. Amid the diversity of meditative practices, there is the deep unity found in listening for God's guidance and presence. For those who regularly meditate, the briefest evocation of their focus word awakens them to peace and joy, and may even calm their cardiovascular system. Like the Christian mystic Brother Lawrence, we may discover that the time spent working in the kitchen, answering e-mail, attending a business meeting, or putting a child to bed reveals God's care as deeply as specifically religious rituals such as worship or communion.

On the pages that follow, we offer five meditative techniques that focus specifically on a particular area of spiritual growth or state of mind to open you to the possibility of greater spiritual evolution in certain areas of your life.

There is one piece of advice we would like to offer before you begin: Like everything else in the spiritual journey, you will need to be patient with your meditative practice. You will need to be gentle with your own imperfections, as you seek to be patient toward the imperfections of others. Many beginning meditation students despair because their minds constantly wander during their meditation sessions. The best antidote to the wandering mind is simply a graceful response and a commitment to the regular practice of meditation. Meditation is a gift from God that can bring wholeness to your life, even if you don't see immediate results. Practice always makes "better." The more you meditate, the more fulfilling your experiences will be.

❀ *LOVINGKINDNESS MEDITATION*

This is a meditation to promote the healing of a relationship with someone who has wronged you, or with someone you may have wronged. It is a meditation that acknowledges both the boulders and the beauty, the fear and the love, in ourselves and in others. It is a meditation that looks for the Divine in each other, that seeks to understand anger and alienation as a cry for help.

- Begin your meditation by recalling someone toward whom you feel great gratitude or love. Imagine your feelings of love and connection sweeping over this person.

- Then, recall another friend toward whom you have feelings of kindness and care, and let your feelings of love radiate toward that person as well.

- Next, recall a difficult person in your life, one toward whom you feel anger, hatred, or fear. Focus on this one with whom you identify great pain or hurt. Let Divine love also radiate from your heart to this person.

- Then, to each of these persons, express the following benedictions:

  "As I wish to be free from danger and achieve safety, so may you be free from danger and achieve safety."

"As I wish to have happiness, so may you have happiness."

"As I wish to have good health and be free from physical or mental pain, so may you have good health and be free from physical or mental pain."

"As I wish to have peace of mind, so may you have peace of mind."

• Now, pause a moment and feel yourself surrounded by God's love. Allow this Eternal love to protect you and dissolve any anger or hatred you feel into warmth and patience toward yourself or others. As you have wished others well, now take time to wish yourself well. Let your heart be filled with lovingkindness toward yourself as you open yourself to the Divine Presence with these words:

"May I be healed, at peace and happy, free from pain and suffering, free from anger, hatred, and fear, filled with Divine joy and love."

• Toward a spouse, child, beloved friend, or even an enemy, continue your prayer of kindness and affirmation with the words:

"May you be healed, at peace and happy, free from pain and suffering, free from anger, hatred, and fear, filled with Divine joy and love."

• Conclude by focusing on the thought that all life is connected and that your happiness is intimately related to the happiness of the strangers and the enemies with which you share the planet.

❀ *FORGIVENESS MEDITATION*

This is a meditation to heal the hurt someone has caused you, or you have inflicted on someone else. It is a meditation to transform pain to love by placing your feelings in the larger perspective of God's love for all creation. It is a meditation to make a choice to forgive.

- Start by taking time to relax into God's presence. Feel yourself surrounded by Divine patience, care, and protection. Know that you are loved just as you are, without condition or expectation. Allow any ambient anger or hatred you feel toward others to be dissolved in the ocean of Divine love.

- With each breath, inhale the warmth of Divine companionship. Breathe in Divine patience and feel the spaciousness of your open heart as it reflects God's love. Let God's forgiveness flow into your life and out into the world.

- Now, feel your body and release any tension or tightness that you may feel as a result of anger or resentment. Let go of the pride that holds on to resentment. Allow the pain of old hurts to fade away as you place it in God's loving hands. Let go of your burdens by placing them in Divine care, where you are safe, strong, and loved.

- As you think of one who has hurt you, remember the pain you felt at the time or have harbored until now. Ask God to assist you in the process of forgiveness. With God as your companion, imagine saying to the one who has hurt you, "I forgive you. We can begin again."

- Now let the love and compassion of God surround you once more, cleansing any pain you may feel as result of any hurt you have caused. Let go of your judgment of yourself, and replace it with compassion and understanding.

♦ In your imagination, turn to the person you have hurt, whether intended or accidental. As you feel your regret for the pain you may have caused, ask that person for forgiveness. Accept God's forgiveness for any suffering you have caused and ask God to enable you to bring healing to this situation.

♦ Conclude this meditation by experiencing God's forgiveness for yourself and the other for the harm that has been done and the failure to live up to God's dream for your life. Commit yourself to personal transformation, to forgiveness and reconciliation.

❀ GUARDIAN ANGEL MEDITATION

For people who are more visually oriented, meditations that involve images or personages may be more life-transforming. Many have found this Guardian Angel Meditation a source of comfort in times of need and challenge. This is a meditation to help you experience a greater sense of God's presence in times of transition. It is a way of discovering that you are surrounded by Divine care and guided by Divine inspiration every step of the way.

♦ After a time of personal quiet and centering, in which you open yourself to God's presence in your life, first imagine the angel Michael—the angel of love and kindness—on your left side. Ask Michael to infuse you with love and kindness for all beings, as well as a feeling of Divine compassion and companionship. If you are alienated from any persons, ask Michael to enable Divine forgiveness to flow through you.

- Then imagine the angel Gabriel—the angel of strength and courage—on your right side. Ask Gabriel to help you overcome fear and anxiety as you entrust your life to God. If there are any specific areas of stress in your life, invite God's messenger Gabriel to bring peace to your heart and mind by reminding you that, at all times and places, you are in God's hands.

- After a few moments, invite Raphael—the angel of healing—to stand behind you, bringing Divine wholeness to your body, mind, and spirit. As you name any illness or problem facing you, ask Raphael to awaken you to the Divine energies of restoration that heal us in life and death.

- Then imagine Uriel—the angel of light—standing right in front of you, infusing you with Divine insight and understanding, and illuminating your own particular challenges.

- Feel the presence of these four messengers of God. Call on each of them to give you a vision of God's dream for your life and the courage to embody that Divine dream.

- Finally, imagine Divine Radiance—in the form of Jesus of Nazareth, or the light of the world, or the *Shekinah*, or the feminine aspect of God—flowing through your whole being, body, mind, spirit, and emotions. Allow this Holy Light to permeate and surround you with God's love, encompass you with inner peace, and awaken you to an undeniable sense of God's care and protection. God wants you to have abundant life. Help is all around you.

- Close by contemplating the words of Psalm 91:11-12: "For [God] will command [the] angels concerning you to guard you in all your ways. On their hands they will bear you up, so that you will not dash your foot against a stone."

❀ *MEANING OF LIFE MEDITATION*

In times of crisis, this mediation can give you new insight about who you are and how you can most creatively respond to the challenging events of your life. It is an opportunity to discover the movements of God within the many events of your life and find renewed spiritual energy.

- Take a few moments to be still, opening yourself to the quiet place where your voice and God's voice blend together as one. With this prayer, ask that deepest part of your being to reveal what is truly most important in your life:

  > "O Eternal One,
  > help me find the enduring truths of life.
  > Let my every word and action be directed toward
  > life's ultimate goals.
  > How eager I am to face you, my Creator.
  > Help me devote my days
  > to prepare for the moment
  > when I will meet you.
  > How I long to come into your Presence!
  > Liberate me from my fantasies and illusions,
  > set me free to be your partner in Creation.
  > From the unreal, lead me to the Real,
  > from darkness lead me to Light,
  > from death lead me to immortality."

- Sit quietly and listen for the still, small voice of God that constantly speaks to your deepest self. Ask the Holy One for the ability to discern the Divine voice amid all the other voices of life. Listen for the intuitions, dreams, and insights that God is revealing in your life.

❀ *A SPIRITUAL ROAD MAP TO THE FUTURE*

This is a meditation to explore imaginatively the road ahead.

- Take time to silently open yourself to God's guidance and insight.
- As you look at your life today, imagine the spiritual horizon that lies before you. Where do you want to go in the future? What images of the future energize you—in terms of vocation, recreation, creativity, health, wholeness, and spirituality?
- Ask for Divine guidance in discerning what images of the future are most life-transforming. Imagine yourself with God as your companion as you journey toward the future. See yourself, like the legendary Abraham and Sarah, and Ruth and Naomi, leaving the familiar and journeying toward the Divine horizon of your life.
- Thank God for being your companion in the past, present, and future. Place the unknown future in Divine hands as you invite God to lead you each step of the way. Ask God to give you the courage of Queen Esther to respond to your calling in "just such a time as this."
- In the spirit of John Henry Newman's prayer, turn the future over to God with the words: "Lead, kindly light amid the encircling gloom, the far shore, I do not ask to see, just one step enough for me."

The Power of Imagination

The Bible is a record of God's surprising imagination: the childless Abraham and Sarah become the parents of a nation; the stammering Moses becomes the spokesperson of liberation; youthful Jeremiah becomes a prophet to a complacent nation; a young girl becomes the mother of God's Holy Child; the most rabid persecutor of the first Christians, Saul of Tarsus, has a vision, receives a new name, and becomes the greatest proclaimer of the new religious movement.

To persons of faith, around every corner a "burning bush" or an angelic messenger can reveal Divine guidance. Every voice can be a summons to begin a Holy Adventure. Yet in the words of William Blake, for most of us, the doors of perception remain bolted and locked. The focus of mind essential for everyday activity often screens out the deeper realities of life. While we are tempted to limit reality to what we see with the five senses, faith suggests a deeper understanding of reality, embracing not only the information of the five senses but also the mystical moments of transfiguration that illumine everyday life. As the Zen Buddhists note, before enlightenment, we "chop wood and carry water." After enlightenment, we still "chop wood and carry water," but now our daily tasks are done as a Holy Adventure in partnership with God. Even the simplest actions are charged with wonder and beauty.

Like the lion who was raised among goats, we often forget who we truly are. With a holy imagination, we can see more in ourselves than meets the eye. Holy imagination is one path to opening the doors of our perception, to experiencing an alternative reality. Through holy imagination, we can see angels in the boulders of our lives and discover in ourselves courageous lions where once were frightened goats.

Visualization exercises can help us to look in the mirror of our lives—and through the eyes of God—to see courage, strength, and power. Visualization exercises can help us expand our minds, liberate us from unhealthy thought patterns, and invite us to new ways of living. A positive mental picture can send messages of success, well-being, and wholeness to our mind and body that can enable us to achieve what we once thought was impossible. In the pages that follow, we offer seven visualizations that invite you to identify your deepest desires in light of God's aim for your life.

❋ *VISUALIZATION FOR RENEWED SELF-ESTEEM*

This is a simple visualization exercise that can help restore your sense of self-worth.

- Take a few moments simply to rest in Divine love.
- Visualize God's love flowing through you. Experience the depth of God's love for you. Feel the energy and power that arises from letting this love flow through you, clearing away dark clouds of doubt and fear, revealing and enhancing your true nature as a child of God, created in the Divine image and endowed with infinite worth.
- Reflect on the truth that you are God's beloved child, with a destiny beyond your imagination.

❋ *VISUALIZATION FOR COURAGE IN A DIFFICULT SITUATION*

This is a visualization to help you prepare for a difficult encounter or a situation about which you are feeling anxious. It is an exercise in what the early Christian teacher Paul describes as "putting on the armor of God."

• Take time to relax in a comfortable position. Breathe gently, calming your body and mind.

• Imagine the upcoming encounter or situation that you dread. What is the nature of the encounter? What feelings do you have toward those who are involved in this encounter?

• Take a moment to look at yourself from a new perspective. See that you are surrounded by invisible, yet impenetrable, spiritual armor. This armor of light protects you and gives you confidence in life. While you are surrounded by this invisible armor, nothing can hurt you. How do you feel knowing this?

• Now take a moment to see the deepest reality of the other(s) involved in this situation. Visualize a conversation in which you stand in your personal truth even as you listen to the truths of the other. What do you need to say to affirm yourself and bring conciliation to the situation? See your own deepest reality as God's beloved, gifted, and resourceful child. Let the encounter unfold with grace and success.

• Conclude by thanking God for always surrounding you and those you love.

❦ *VISUALIZATION FOR RELIEF OF BURDENS*

For many of us, the present is weighed down by the heavy burdens of the past that rob us of the joy of life. Bound to the past, we feel little hope for future transformation. Through healing imagination, we can let go life's burdens and awaken to a future filled with hope and anticipation. This visualization can help you release the past and open the future by placing your burdens in the hands of God.

- Begin in a quiet place, either sitting or lying with your eyes closed.

- As you briefly review your life, reflect on a particular burden that weighs you down. (These burdens may be spiritual, psychological, emotional, or relational in nature; they can involve regrets about the past as well as anxiety about the future.) Feel their weight upon your life. See you how they have robbed you of the joy of life.

- In your imagination, visualize these burdens as heavy boulders that you carry around in a backpack. Feel how these boulders weigh you down with each step.

- See yourself walking, burdened by your heavy load. Imagine that you come upon a stone table where you are greeted by the Holy One. Visualize the Holy One in whatever form speaks to your experience today. The Holy One bids you take off your backpack and sit nearby. As you sit with the Holy One, you are invited to take each boulder, and whatever it symbolizes in your life, and place it in the hands of God.

- With each boulder you place in God's hands, feel the burdens of life becoming lighter and lighter. Continue the process until you have placed each and every boulder in God's care.

- As you pick up your backpack, you notice it is empty. How does it feel to carry such a light load? How does it feel to share your burdens with God?

- Visualize yourself walking into the future with lightness and grace.

- Conclude by thanking God for allowing you to place your burdens in Divine Hands.

❦ *VISUALIZATION FOR GUIDANCE FOR THE DAY*

This is a visualization you can use at the beginning and end of each day to claim God's guiding hand on your life.

• AS YOU WAKEN IN THE MORNING, re-affirm the words of Scripture, "This is the day that [God] has made; let us rejoice and be glad in it" (Psalm 118:24). Begin the day with thanksgiving for the amazing gift of life and the possibilities that lie ahead of you in the next twenty-four hours. Take time to gently look at the day ahead, imaging your goals for the day.

• Take a moment to ponder the challenges you may face in the day ahead. As you anticipate each event, image God as your companion and friend. Visualize Divine guidance inspiring you in each situation. With God beside you, see yourself speaking words of truth, clarity, love, and insight. Imagine the day ahead as an opportunity to bring joy to others and to experience happiness and hope.

• See one particular person to whom Divine guidance directs you. In the quiet of the morning, ponder what words or actions will bring joy or healing to this person.

• Let yourself contemplate, for a few moments, these truths: Wherever I go today, God will be with me; in every life situation, God offers me abundant resources for growth and love.

. . .

• AT DAY'S END, take a few moments to thank God for being your guide and companion throughout the day.

• If you are carrying any regrets or burdens from the day, place them in Divine hands. If you have hurt anyone, ask for Divine forgiveness and guidance in making amends. If another has hurt you, feel the pain and then place it in God's hands for strength to love and forgive.

- As you close your eyes, ask for Divine protection as you sleep and for guidance through dreams and inspirations in the night.

- Place the day ahead in God's hands with expectations of joy, adventure, and healing. Ask God to enable you to wake tomorrow with hope and vitality.

❀ VISUALIZATION FOR RECONCILIATION IN A DIFFICULT RELATIONSHIP

This is a visualization that can help bring forgiveness and reconciliation in a situation of interpersonal conflict.

- Find a gentle, comfortable position. Take a few minutes to breathe in God's restful companionship.

- Visualize the person in your life with whom there is a conflict. Explore the conflict and its impact on you. Consider also its impact on the other.

- Image this person in terms of a jagged boulder, noting the unique type of boulder that he or she is.

- Now look a bit deeper, letting your eyes see beyond the jagged exterior. Look for the deeper reality beyond the jagged exterior. What holiness is the boulder hiding? What beauty lies beneath? What potential for growth can arise out of your relationship with this person?

- Open your eyes to the reality that God wants you to see in this person.

- Conclude by asking God's help in enabling you to bring forth the holiness in this person.

❀ *VISUALIZATION FOR FORGIVENESS*

This visualization, which is a variation of the Matthew and Dennis Linn's "healing of memories," can help you forgive someone who has hurt you and move on with your life.[15]

+ Start by quieting yourself and offering a prayer for God's presence in the situation that you will be imaging.

+ In your mind, go back down the trail of pain to the situation that troubles you.

+ Look at the situation from many perspectives, feeling the hurt and the pain, and experiencing the actions of the other person.

+ Prayerfully invite God (or Christ or an angelic being) to be your companion in this situation. Share your feelings with God and ask God for strength to forgive and let go of the pain. What does the Divine One say to you?

+ Experience God's care for you and the one who has hurt you. With God as your companion, reach out to the other in forgiveness. After this act of forgiveness, place the past in God's care with the prayer that God carry the pain from now on. (If the pain is too great for reconciliation, simply turn the pain over to God, letting God do the healing through your unconscious mind.)

+ Conclude with a prayer of thanksgiving for God's healing presence.

15 Dennis and Matthew Linn, *Healing Life's Hurts* (New York: Paulist Press, 1977) and *Healing of Memories* (New York: Paulist Press, 1984).

✿ *VISUALIZATION FOR WELL-BEING*

This is a visualization that joins your well-being with the well-being of another person in the light of God. While the goal of healing imagination is, first of all, your own transformation, in the spirit of the "butterfly effect," as you change your image of the other, he or she may begin to unconsciously change as well.

* Take time to relax, closing your eyes as you sit in a comfortable position.

* Breathe deeply, experiencing the Love in which you live, move, and have your being.

* With each breath, experience God's light entering your whole being.

* See this healing light filling you from head to toe, bringing wholeness to every aspect of your life. As the light permeates your body, beginning with your head and working its way downward, if you have a particular need in mind, body, or spirit, let the light surround, illuminate, and permeate that part of your life.

* Now, as you breathe in this healing light, see it surrounding and permeating the life of another. See the light bringing healing to their known and unknown hurts and limitations, wholeness to every aspect of their lives.

* As you conclude, experience the healing light joining the two of you in an unbroken circle of love, in which your well-being and their well-being is united in God's loving care.

* Close with a moment of thanksgiving for God's healing light in your life.

The Perspective of Affirmation

Our attitudes can bring us joy or sorrow. A mindful journey through the day will reveal how often we are imprisoned by negative feelings about ourselves and others. We are created for love, prosperity, wholeness, and creativity, but we often see ourselves as weak and ineffectual. We internalize the negativity of our culture and family of origin. We harbor negative self-images that condition and limit our possibilities. Our speech is dominated by words and phrases such as, "I can't," "If only," "It's impossible," "I'm too old," "I'm too young," or "I'll never be able to."

Often these negative images are a vestige of some earlier statement by a parent, teacher, or authority figure that we have let determine our gifts and talents. We may not dance in public because someone made fun of us at the junior high school dance thirty years ago. We may start to sweat when we are asked to speak publicly because in grade school we fumbled an easy word in the spelling bee. We may settle for "second best" at work and relationships because we feel unworthy of success and true love.

Our minds need healing in order for us to become the spiritual lions God intends us to be, as the great Christian spiritual leader the apostle Paul proclaimed: "Do not be not conformed to this world, but be transformed by the renewing of your minds" (Romans 12:2). That same message was embodied by the prophets who imagined a world of peace, of the lion and lamb as companions, though war was all around them. The Bible is a book of spiritual affirmations. Just think of the familiar words of the first chapter of Genesis (v. 26): "Let us make humankind in our image." Regardless of our current self-image, this verse affirms for each of us:

- *"I am created in God's image."*
- *"My body and mind are the gift of a wise and loving God."*
- *"Only God can define my true nature, and God says I am God's beloved creation."*

Or consider a version of Psalm 23:

- *"God, you are my shepherd, I shall not want. You make me lie down in green pastures; you lead me beside still waters, you restore my soul. You lead me in right paths for your name's sake. Even though I walk through the darkest valley, I fear no evil; for you are with me; your rod and your staff they comfort me. You prepare a table before me in the presence of my enemies; you anoint my head with oil. My cup overflows. Surely goodness and mercy shall follow me all the days of my life, and I shall dwell in the house of the God my whole life long."*

What a wonderful treasure of positive affirmations there are in these few verses:

- *"God gives me everything I need."*
- *"God is constantly restoring my soul."*
- *"God is with me in the darkest night"*
- *"I am not afraid, for God is protecting me."*
- *"My cup overflows with joy, love, prosperity."*
- *"I live in God's presence."*

Jesus told his disciples, "You are the light of the world" (Matthew 5:14), and the first verses of John's Gospel proclaim that "the light shines in the darkness, and the darkness did not overcome it" (John 1:5). These verses are affirmations of our true identity as a beloved child of God:

- *"I am the light of the world."*
- *"God's light shines in the darkest moments of my life."*
- *"God's light constantly guides and enlightens me."*

Spiritual affirmations can help heal mind, body, and relationships. Positive affirmations are a tangible way to experience God's abundant life and claim our personal resources in the context of chronic or life-threatening illness, tragedy, unemployment, financial reversals, bereavement, or depression. The repetition of spiritual words awakens the conscious mind to new beliefs and behaviors and, through regular practice, cleanses the unconscious mind of thoughts and feelings that place unnecessary limits on us. While at first glance, affirmations seem counter to reality, they actually reveal a deeper reality of ourselves than the one we are currently experiencing. Affirmations do not deny life's challenges and our own imperfections. Rather, they place the negative and limiting in a new perspective—God's vision of who we are!

Using positive spiritual affirmations simply involves making non-judgmental statements about yourself and the world. In the rest of this chapter, we offer some affirmations that we have found helpful in encouraging a positive attitude toward life and our possibilities as children of a loving God. We hope they will inspire you to create spiritual affirmations of your own as a means of embodying God's presence in your life.

❀ *AFFIRMATIONS FOR HEALING*

The biblical tradition is a wellspring of healing affirmations:

- *"I am created in God's image."* (Genesis 1:26)
- *"God's spirit is with me wherever I go."* (Psalm 139:7-12)
- *"God is protecting me."* (Psalm 1:1-6)
- *"God's light shines in me."* (Matthew 5:14)
- *"Nothing can separate me from God's love."* (Romans 8:39)
- *"My faith is healing me."* (Mark 5:28)
- *"God is supplying my deepest needs."* (Philippians 4:19)

❀ *AFFIRMATIONS FOR HEALTH, WELL-BEING, AND SELF-ESTEEM*

General affirmations can enhance your health, well-being, and self-esteem:

- *"My body is the temple of God. I eat wisely and exercise regularly."*
- *"God inspires me in everything I do."*
- *"God's wisdom guides each step I take."*
- *"I am blessed to be a blessing."*
- *"I greet everyone with a kind word and a smile."*
- *"I see the holiness in everyone I meet and bring it out through my care for them."*

❀ AFFIRMATIONS FOR HOPEFULNESS, SERENITY, AND COURAGE

Specific affirmations can nurture feelings of hopefulness, serenity, and courage:

+ *"I awaken to a day of joy and prosperity."*
+ *"I let go of limitations and open to God's limitless possibilities."*
+ *"The God within me finds expression in feelings of self-esteem."*
+ *"God has given me everything I need to succeed, prosper, and serve my neighbor."*
+ *"God is with me in the storms of life."*
+ *"I face the storms of life with serenity and courage."*
+ *"I express Divine courage in challenging situations."*
+ *"God's angels surround and protect me and those I love."*
+ *"Divine creativity constantly flows through me, and I share it with others."*
+ *"I am a calm expression of Divine love."*
+ *"My words and thoughts express Divine love and creativity."*

❀ AFFIRMATIONS OF SURRENDER

Affirmations of surrender may help you open yourself to God's guidance and activity in your life:

+ *"I trust in God's help; everything will be for the best."*
+ *"God is working for the best in this situation."*
+ *"I align myself with Divine wisdom and let God lead the way."*
+ *"In all things, God is working for good."*

In times of great difficulty, affirmations can help us experience a sense of protection and wholeness. The affirmation "nothing can separate me from the love of God" may become, "The fluctuating stock market can't separate me from the love of God," or "The pain of separation and divorce can't separate me from the love of God." There is no dividing line between the sacred and secular. We can use affirmations for every aspect of life. While there is no certainty in the world today, one thing we know for certain: God wants us to experience abundance in every aspect of our lives. The Holy One wants us break open the boulders that blind us to the angel within.

We are not victims of the world around us. While we cannot fully control the events that shape our lives, we have been given tools of spiritual transformation. In awakening to God's dynamic presence through prayer, meditation, healing imagination, and spiritual affirmations, we can begin to heal ourselves, our neighbors, our families, and to mend our planet.

CHAPTER FIVE

Mending Ourselves and Our Planet

EVERY year, former professional football player Steve Fitzhugh takes a group of inner-city teenagers to the woods far from Washington, D.C., in order to "show them the face of God." No longer surrounded by gangs, drug addicts, or hopelessness, these young people experience the wonder of a starry night—often for the first time. As they gaze at the heavens, a whole new world of possibilities emerges for them. For some of them, the experience is life-changing. In the immensity of the night sky, they see their lives from a new perspective. They experience a spaciousness of spirit that cannot be confined by the opinions of others, the burdens of past behavior, or limited images of the future.

Like these inner-city teenagers, we, too, need to be freed from the unnecessary limits that dominate our thoughts and expectations. We, too, need to see the face of God in the infinity of the heavens. We, too, need to see the possibilities before us.

146 🏵 *Mending the World*

In this book, we have invited you to imagine God's vision for your life and to become a conscious partner in God's Holy Adventure. We have asked you to look for the angels in yourself and others. In this chapter, we challenge you to experience God's dream for the planet.

God's dream includes not only the fulfillment of our lives but also imagining new possibilities for the earth. God's Shalom weaves together the personal and the planetary. In the ecology of life, our destinies are joined. Wholeness anywhere contributes to healing everywhere. Shalom is the vision of that wholeness amid life's personal and planetary struggles and challenges.

At first glance, God's dream for our planet seems utterly impossible. As we ponder the daily news, our minds are filled with images of violence, manipulation, deceit, and alienation. Only with the greatest difficulty can we imagine a world of peace, prosperity, justice, and unity. We are certainly not the first people to experience the tension between God's dream for the world and the current state of affairs. Take a moment to meditate upon God's vision for creation as found in the words of the prophet Isaiah:

> They shall beat their swords into plowshares, and their spears into pruning hooks; nation shall not lift up sword against nation, neither shall they learn war any more. (Isaiah 2:4)

> The wolf shall lie down with the lamb, and the leopard shall lie down with the kid; the calf and the lion and the fatling together; and a little child shall lead them. . . . They will not hurt or destroy on all my holy mountain; for the earth shall be full of the knowledge of the

Lord as the waters cover the sea. (Isaiah 11:6,9)

Listen, also, to the jubilant words of Mary the mother of Jesus as she envisages her role in bringing about God's reign of justice:

[God] has lifted up the lowly . . . and has filled the hungry with good things. (Luke 1:52-53)

God's dream for the world is conceived precisely in the tension of love and hate, threat and security, abundance and scarcity, life and death, and justice and oppression. Like the prophets of ancient Israel and the teacher from Nazareth, we know that many boulders stand in the way of our dream of a new heaven and a new earth. Faced with the jagged edges of global warming, ecological degradation, world hunger and starvation, inadequate health care, and terrorist threats, we are tempted to focus only on our own spiritual growth and the welfare of our immediate neighbors. Yet the vision of Shalom challenges us to become people who join our spiritual growth with others for the transformation of the world.

Nothing is more essential to the transformation of the world than our willingness to transform our own spiritual lives. Yet our spiritual quest takes us beyond the practices of meditation and prayer and plunges us into the maelstrom of conflict and imperfection. Moses and Jesus had to leave the spiritual inspiration of the mountain top to bring healing and justice to their communities. Queen Esther, despite her fears of losing her throne, had to break her silence and speak out on behalf of the Jewish people. Our

spiritual commitments embrace our jobs, families, marriages and significant relationships, sexuality and
parenting, economics, eating habits, and politics. With the
founders of the Kirkridge Retreat Center in Pocono Mountains of Pennsylvania, we are called both literally and meta-
phorically to "picket and pray," to seek justice through the
path of faith, courage, love, and forgiveness.

As Martin Luther King, Jr., affirmed, we are all
bound together in the intricate web of life. We cannot find
wholeness and abundance on our own. We cannot hide behind missile defense systems or gated communities. We
need the health of others in order to experience our own authentic wholeness. We need healthy communities and nations in order to sustain our spiritual and physical
well-being. Most of all, apart from the commitment to planetary and social healing, our own quest for healing and
wholeness will eventually fail.

Throughout this book, we have mentioned the "butterfly effect," the impact of small choices that transform the
world. Yet even as we dream of fluttering our own spiritual
wings of transformation, we are overwhelmed by the image
of millions of monarch butterflies dying in Mexico, the victims of the interplay of deforestation and the cool weather
of February 2002. We must admit that we can destroy as
well as create. The beauty of monarch butterfly and the maj-
esty of God's presence in each one of us is fragile and easily
destroyed.

As stewards of the earth in whose hands rest the
survival of the oceans, forests, butterflies, fellow species,
and our future children, our call to Shalom includes bringing forth the angels from the boulders of our current ecological, economic, social, and political realities. God's love
embraces the endangered species, the starving child, the

homeless person, and the seeker within our faith traditions as well as the adherents of other faith traditions. Shalom is profoundly global, calling us to become God's partners in mending a world of brokenness.

Think for a moment of the Hebraic spiritual leader Samuel. See yourself unexpectedly encountering the Holy One. As a young boy, Samuel heard a voice in the night, persistently calling, "Samuel, Samuel." He went to the high priest Eli, thinking that he was being summoned by his spiritual superior, but the aged priest sent him back to bed. Again and again, the voice came to Samuel until, finally, he cried out to God, "Speak . . . your servant is listening" (1 Samuel 3:10).

Could it be the voice of God is calling us in the restlessness of our dreams, imagination, and conscience? God may awaken us through our regular spiritual practices of centering prayer, biblical affirmations, or healing imagery. But the call also pushes us beyond our private relationship with the Holy One. The call of God comes through the face of a starving child and mounds of dying monarch butterflies. God's voice resounds in the battered spouse and the elder who is unable to afford adequate health care. In the midst of all other voices, God calls us by name, showing us the pain and the hope of the world. Listen! Can you hear a voice echoing through all the other voices of your life? Open your eyes! Can you see God disguised in the least of these? Could it be that we, like Queen Esther, are called to mend the world in "just such a time as this"? As the Roman Catholic monk Thomas Merton asserts, we need to join both contemplation and action in facing the challenges of the day.

Once again, we need to remember the story of a rural gathering in which Jesus of Nazareth spoke to thousands of men and women (John 6:1-14). As evening drew near, Jesus' disciples came to him with an urgent request: "Look at all these people. The day is long and we're far from town, and there's nothing to eat! How shall we feed them?" We can imagine that a call for food went through the throng, but no one admitted to having brought dinner except a humble child whose mother had sent a modest basket, filled only with five loaves of bread and two small fish. No doubt laughter went through the crowd as the boy brought his lunch to Jesus. "How can such a paltry quantity feed such a multitude?" sneered the scoffers. But, to their amazement, Jesus fed thousands from that small offering.

Perhaps, the boy's generosity unleashed a first-century version of the "butterfly effect" and challenged others in the crowd to share the food that they previously reserved for themselves. Or, perhaps, Jesus transformed a few loaves into a banquet by joining the creative power of Divine imagination with the holy energy that flowed through his life. However we explain it, a miracle—a release of unexpected Divine energy—occurred, and the multitudes feasted on food for body and spirit as they awakened to the Divine abundance that had been present all the time. That day Jesus saw abundance where others saw scarcity, hope where others saw poverty and failure. From the boulder of disbelief and impossibility, Jesus released the angel of hope and generosity that fed a multitude then—and can nourish our planet today.

Walt Whitman once stated, "To me, everything is a miracle." Take some time now—or later today—to let yourself envision the miracle of Shalom:

The Miracle of Shalom

* Give yourself a moment of quiet simply to rest in God's loving light. With each breath you take, imagine God's light infusing your body, mind, and spirit. Experience this holy light surrounding and protecting you.

* Then let God's light flow through your life to the wider world. See the Divine light surround and permeate your spouse and children, your best friend, a co-worker. Image God's healing surrounding a stranger you may have noticed at the store or on your way to work.

* Let the loving light of God expand further beyond your circle of friends and acquaintances to embrace the person with whom you feel most uncomfortable; the political leader who represents for you the worst aspects of your nation's political and social life; the terrorists in the Al-Qaeda network.

* Experience God's light permeating the non-human world of monarch butterflies, chimpanzees, dolphins, and eagles (and the dog and cat who may be your daily companions).

* See God's light extending from your household to your community (and especially to those parts of the community you routinely avoid), to prisons and jails, to the capital of your state and your nation, to your nation, and then joining the planet and illuminating the entire cosmos in a great light of love and healing.

* Imagine God's healing light joining you with all things, and embracing all things in an intricately woven tapestry of relationships.

- Now, take your meditation and visualization a bit further. Ground it in a commitment to action. As you visualize the earth and its many communities, where do you feel called to loving service? Who needs your healing touch? What gifts do you have that respond to the world's needs?

- Focus a few minutes on some area in your family, community, nation, and world. In what ways can you concretely act to mend the microcosm of your immediate community? Remember that, because wholeness anywhere contributes to healing everywhere, your act will contribute to healing the macrocosm of the nation and planet.

- As you pray for guidance, commit yourself to loving action.

Each of us has a unique role in mending the earth. We can make a difference precisely because we live in a world of relationships and connections where we constantly shape one another's experiences. We are not isolated atoms or self-made individuals. We arise from an intricate ecology of relationships. Our lives are our contribution, for better or worse, to the world beyond ourselves. Our prayers radiate across the universe—and so do our commitments to seek justice and healing in the world by contacting our elected representatives, volunteering in a soup kitchen or food bank, running a marathon or biking across town to raise money to respond to world hunger or for research related to cancer and AIDS, or simply through blessing our neighbors as we write a check or place a bill in the offering plate. We may, much to our surprise, be the answer to someone's deepest longing or need. Our ordinary acts of kindness may be healing catalysts for a child, spouse, friend, or stranger. Our political involvements can shape the future of millions for joy or sorrow. By the spirit of Shalom, we can add unique beauty to the world around us.

But, more than that, our conscious commitment to bring beauty and love into the world is our greatest gift to God. In the spirit of Jesus' words from Matthew 25:40, "Just as you did it to one of the least of these who are members of my family, you did it to me," we are challenged to do something beautiful for God in every encounter.

No one is excluded from the great adventure of love. Abused children can learn surprising love in the company of elders for whom relationship means affirmation. Wounded marriages can begin again as couples rediscover the angel within the boulders of their lives and commit themselves to healing through spiritual growth, warm embraces, truthful sharing, words of love, new behaviors, and forgiveness. Burned-out executives can discover flaming passion of creativity by embracing new images of themselves. They can discover an abundance that will never fail as they share their largesse with others and commit their organizations to behaviors that bring life to society and the planet. Senior adults can experience new meaning as they explore new patterns of thought and behavior, and share their wisdom with the next generation. The dying can live more fully than they had previously imagined by making each moment an epiphany through their commitment to compassion, love, and forgiveness.

As the African-American slaves discovered on their impossible journey from slavery to freedom, God makes a way when there seems to be no way. There are no ultimate dead ends in the spiritual journey. When we align ourselves with the vision of Shalom in partnership with God and our fellow creatures, we discover infinite possibilities for living and loving. We see the face of God everywhere. As we rejoice in the uniqueness of each life and the abundance of God's love, we recognize that there is no one path to fulfillment or spiritual practice for all persons or age groups. We are God's beloved children, and our unique light joins with countless other light bearers to bring healing to all creation.

The Holy Adventure leads us to new horizons of love and service, regardless of our current circumstances. As both Jewish and Christian spiritual guides have recognized, the only adequate name for God is love—the intimate, innovative, personal, and cosmic Love that heals the sick, gives life to the dying, and opens our hearts to the cry of all creation. Intimate beyond our imagination, God loves us into life and leads us to greater love—one encounter at a time. The love of God invites us to see each moment as an adventure that begins with the individual and extends to the cosmos. In every encounter a quiet, but persistent voice calls us to become the Creator's loving companions in mending the planet. Can you hear that adventurous and loving voice in your hopes and dreams?

The Holy Adventure

Take time to let the circumstances of the wider world call you to prayer and action. As you read the news or watch it on television, consider these questions:

• Where is your heart broken? What needs call out to you? Take time to surround those needs in prayer, meditation, imagery, and affirmation. Ask God to reveal how you can be a healing presence in addressing this need.

- Take notice of your feelings. Are you beginning to feel anxious, afraid, or angry? Are you beginning to draw lines between the faithful and the infidel, your community and its enemies? Do you feel hatred toward some of the personalities involved in the story? Or do you simply feel powerless to make any difference?

- Once again, let these boulders call you to prayer, meditation, visualization, and affirmation. See the angel in the boulder of those you hate or mistrust. See them as children of God, deserving love as well as justice. Ask God to show guide your country to be a force for good rather evil, for reconciliation rather than alienation, in addressing global issues. If fear arises, turn to an affirmation of faith, such as: *"I am in God's hands. I am safe and secure"* or *"Nothing can separate me from the love of God."*

- Visualize yourself surrounded by God's protective light and extend that light to those from whom you are alienated.

- Commit yourself to some form of loving action to complement your emerging spiritual awareness.

- Remember that your spiritual growth and centeredness is the foundation from which you bring healing to the world. You are not here by accident. In the Divine quest for justice and wholeness, you have a role that is singular and unique. The Holy Adventure calls you.

A Jewish aphorism notes that because God loves stories, God created humankind. The Great Storyteller, whose artistry encompasses universe upon universe, and all creatures in heaven and earth, weaves wisdom and creativity through each of our lives and lives of all things. We are all fellow adventurers in the grand universal story of evolution, surprise, conflict, and reconciliation. We are all on a heroic journey that has no end, an adventure built upon the faith of the ancients and shaping the lives of those who follow us. As you look at your life, ask yourself, "What is my story and where does it fit it with the challenge of planetary transformation? What task of planetary healing lies before me?" The task may not be great in the eyes of the world, but still it is essential because the world is transformed and healed one moment and one person at a time.

When Bruce's son, Matt, was a young child, father and son often read the "Choose Your Own Adventure" book series. As they read together, they found that each choice led to a different outcome: one decision to a palace, the other to a dungeon; one choice to peace, the other to warfare. As we discover the interplay of our inner and outer spiritual journeys, we also "choose our own adventures" amid the challenges of our lives. Our individual and community stories can bring healing to people, species, and to the planet itself.

The story of Shalom is far from ending. God's dream for us and for the world is just getting started. Many adventures lie ahead. As we embody the adventurous spirit of Shalom, mending the world wherever we find ourselves, we will have many spiritual companions. Whatever choices we make, they will lead to new and exciting adventures in the great journey of the universe.

In the Jewish tradition, the task of sculpting angels from the boulders of our communal lives has been given the name of *tikkun olam,* or mending the universe. In Christianity, this same dream of uniting our quest for healing and wholeness with the healing of the planet is referred to as *the reign of God* or *the body of Christ.* To see the world in God's light may seem incredible, but the Jewish and Christian traditions proclaim that this incredible vision is our reality and our ultimate destiny.

As you choose your own Holy Adventure, remember this: You are more creative and powerful than you can imagine. Like the lion raised among goats, you can discover your true nature as a child of God and roar with joy. Go forth with and in the love of God. There is an angel in every boulder just waiting for your strong and loving touch.

Shalom!

REV. BRUCE G. EPPERLY, Ph.D. is Director of Washington Institute for Spirituality and Health, and Adjunct Professor in Theology and Spirituality at Wesley Theological Seminary and Georgetown University School of Medicine. He is the author of seven books, including *God's Touch: Faith, Wholeness, and the Healing Miracles of Jesus* and *The Power of Affirmative Faith: A Spirituality of Personal Transformation.* He is an ordained minister in the United Church of Christ and the Christian Church (Disciples of Christ) and is currently pastor of Townsville Christian Church in Williamsport, Maryland. Dr. Epperly is married to Rev. Dr. Katherine Gould Epperly, pastor of Palisades Community Church in Washington, D.C., and is the father of Matthew Epperly.

RABBI LEWIS D. SOLOMON, an ordained post-denominational rabbi, is the Theodore Rinehart Professor of Business Law at The George Washington University Law School where he has taught for twenty-five years. He is the author of five Judaic books, including *Jewish Spirituality: Revitalizing Judaism for the Twenty-First Century; The Jewish Tradition, Sexuality and Procreation;* and *The Jewish Book of Living and Dying;* and is President of the International Federation of Rabbis, an inclusive professional organization. Rabbi Solomon is married to Dr. Janet Stern Solomon and is the father of Michael Solomon.

Spiritual classics that call to the deep heart's core...

The Haunt of Grace
TED LODER
The "sneaky" ways God surfaces in the middle of everyday life.

Guerrillas of Grace
Prayers for the Battle
TED LODER
One of Innisfree's best-sellers! Tough, beautiful earthy prayers.

My Heart in My Mouth
Prayers for Our Lives
TED LODER
Gutsy, grace-filled prayers that break out of all formulas.

Wrestling the Light
Ache and Awe in the Human-Divine Struggle
TED LODER
Prayers and stories that reflect the depths and joys of the human struggle.

Stumbling Toward God
A Prodigal's Return
MARGARET D. MCGEE
"An offbeat, engagingly written, appealingly uncertain spiritual memoir."—*Publishers Weekly*

Practicing Your Path
A Book of Retreats for an Intentional Life
HOLLY WHITCOMB
Seven retreats for spiritual seekers to rebalance busy days and regain perspective.

The God Between Us
A Spirituality of Relationships
LYN BRAKEMAN
Through midrash, a fresh awareness of how the divine is present to us in the 'between' of human relationships.

Spiritual Lemons
Biblical Women, Irreverent Laughter, and Righteous Rage
LYN BRAKEMAN
Through midrash, the struggles of biblical women reveal that the very places that are difficult are, in fact, places and occasions of grace.